ANYWHERE BUT HERE

ALSO BY CARMEN AGUIRRE

*Blue Box**

*Chile Con Carne and Other Early Plays**

Mexican Hooker #1 and My Other Roles Since the Revolution

*The Refugee Hotel**

Something Fierce: Memoirs of a Revolutionary Daughter

*The Trigger**

* Published by Talonbooks

Anywhere but Here

A PLAY BY
CARMEN AGUIRRE

RAPS CREATED WITH
SHAD KABANGO

TALONBOOKS

Talonbooks
9259 Shaughnessy Street, Vancouver, British Columbia, Canada v6p 6r4
talonbooks.com

Talonbooks is located on xʷməθkʷəẏəm, Sḵwx̱wú7mesh, and səlilwətaʔɬ Lands.

First printing: 2021

Typeset in Minion
Printed and bound in Canada on 100% post-consumer recycled paper

Interior design by Typesmith
Cover artwork conceived by Clayton Baraniuk, designed by Kyra Wittkopf

Talonbooks acknowledges the financial support of the Canada Council for
the Arts, the Government of Canada through the Canada Book Fund, and the
Province of British Columbia through the British Columbia Arts Council and
the Book Publishing Tax Credit.

Rights to produce *Anywhere but Here*, in whole or in part, in any medium
by any group, amateur or professional, are retained by the author. Interested
persons are requested to contact Talonbooks at 9259 Shaughnessy Street,
Vancouver, British Columbia, Canada, v6p 6r4, telephone (toll-free):
1-888-445-4176; email: info@talonbooks.com; website: talonbooks.com.

Library and Archives Canada Cataloguing in Publication

Title: Anywhere but here / Carmen Aguirre.
Names: Aguirre, Carmen, 1967– author.
Description: A play. | Text in English; includes some text in Spanish.
Identifiers: Canadiana 20200375229 | ISBN 9781772012903 (softcover)
Classification: LCC PS8601.G86 A79 2021 | DDC C812/.6—dc23

For all the exiles reaching their way back "home"

"Happiness not in another place, but this place ... not for another hour, but this hour."

— WALT WHITMAN
"A Song for Occupations," *Leaves of Grass* (1855)

PLAYWRIGHT'S PREFACE

Anywhere but Here was in my brain for thirty years. It's based on a series of dreams about exile and cultural identity that I had when I was still in theatre school. I wrote them down in a journal back then, making illustrations alongside the entries. I began taking notes on the play many years later, but always hit a dead end, and it would end up at the back of a drawer.

In 2014, Vancouver's Playwrights Theatre Centre started their Associates program. I pulled the notes out and applied. My idea was accepted, and over the next six years Heidi Taylor, my dramaturge, shepherded *Anywhere but Here* from a mere concept to the full-length play that premiered at the Vancouver Playhouse in February 2020. It was the biggest world premiere of a Latinx Canadian play in Canadian theatre history, a Latinx theatre extravaganza featuring a borderless cast of nine actors of colour, eight of whom were Latinx, led by acclaimed Los Angeles-based Chicanx duo, director Juliette Carrillo and designer Christopher Acebo, in their Canadian debut.

Here's to dreams, and to following them. Here's to dreams that come true thanks to the collective work and sacrifice of so many.

Newen.

PRODUCTION HISTORY

Anywhere but Here was first produced from February 4 to 15, 2020, by Electric Company Theatre in association with Playwrights Theatre Centre and presented with the PuSh International Performing Arts Festival in Vancouver, British Columbia, with the following cast and crew:

MANUEL and others	Nadeem Phillip
LAURA and others	Christine Quintana
LUPE and others	AJ Simmons
CAROLITA	Alexandra Lainfiesta
ARCANGEL and others	Alen Dominguez
TEENAGED GIRL and others	Manuela Sosa
ABUELO and others	Augusto Bitter
YOUNG MAN WITH GUNS and others	Shawn Lall
GENERAL JUANA AZURDUY DE PADILLA and others	Michelle Rios

Director	Juliette Carrillo
Dramaturge	Heidi Taylor
Composer / Music Director	Joelysa Pankanea
Original Recorded Music	Robin Layne, Michael Simpsonelli, and Johnny Wah
Scenic Designer	Christopher Acebo
Costume Designer	Carmen Alatorre
Lighting Designer	Itai Erdal
Sound Designer	Eli Haligua
Projection Designer	Candelario Andrade
Assistant Director	Pedro Chamale
Stage Manager	Joanne P.B. Smith
Production Manager	Adrian Muir
Assistant Stage Manager	Rebecca Mulvihill
Assistant Technical Director	Gustavo Cunha

1

CHARACTERS

The play's characters are played by nine actors. First choice is an all-Latinx cast; second choice is a very diverse cast.

MANUEL, a sexy nerd in his thirties. He has shaggy raven hair and wears black-rimmed Coke-bottle glasses held together by Scotch tape. The actor playing him also plays OLD MAN WITH EGG.

LAURA, a cute hippie in her thirties, a little round, wearing John Lennon glasses. She has long, crazy black curls. The actor playing her also plays STRAWBERRY SELLER.

LUPE, Laura and Manuel's twelve-year-old daughter. Long raven hair. She wears a T-shirt that says, "I Know You Are But What Am I?" The actor playing her also plays the dog EL NEGRO MATAPACOS.

CAROLITA, Lupe's eleven-year-old sister. Barrettes in her long raven hair. Her T-shirt says, "Disco Kid."

ARCANGEL, WALKIE-TALKIE / UNCLE, YOUNG MAN WITH A BALLOON IN HIS HEART, MONARCH BUTTERFLY, all played by one actor.

TEENAGED GIRL, CHICLET SELLER, LUPE'S DOPPEL-GÄNGER, MONARCH BUTTERFLY, all played by one actor.

ABUELO, FUNERAL WREATH SELLER, AUNT LILI, CAROLITA'S DOPPELGÄNGER, LAURA'S UNIVERSITY RESIDENCE GIGGLING FRIEND, all played by one actor.

2

YOUNG MAN WITH GUNS, THE HIPPIE, MAN WITH TV DINNER, FLOOR WAXER, all played by one actor.

GENERAL JUANA AZURDUY DE PADILLA, MONARCH BUTTERFLY, THE VIRGIN CARMEN, all played by one actor.

SETTING

The play takes place on the I-5 Highway in Washington State in 1979, and on the Mexico–United States border in 1979, 1973, 1996, and 2020. These eras occur simultaneously.

PRE-SHOW MUSIC

Let's Groove
performed by Earth, Wind & Fire

Boogie Wonderland
performed by Earth, Wind & Fire with the Emotions

September
performed by Earth, Wind & Fire

Heaven Must Be Missing an Angel
performed by Tavares

Let the Music Play
performed by Barry White

The Hustle
performed by Van McCoy & the Soul City Symphony

Never Knew Love like This Before
performed by Stephanie Mills

This Will Be (An Everlasting Love)
performed by Natalie Cole

You Make Me Feel like Dancing
performed by Leo Sayer

Don't Leave Me This Way
performed by Thelma Houston

Rock with You
performed by Michael Jackson

Act 1

PROLOGUE

*A summer night in 1979. A Chilean house party at
Maria's commune. Barry White's "Love's Theme"
plays full blast. A wordless scene in unabashed
telenovela style unfolds.*

*CAROLITA spies LAURA making out with THE
HIPPIE on a couch.*

LUPE sleeps.

*MANUEL enters. He freaks out. He tries to hit
THE HIPPIE. LAURA gets between them.*

CAROLITA still spies. LUPE still sleeps.

*MANUEL grabs CAROLITA, wakes LUPE up, and
leaves the house with them both.*

"Love's Theme" still plays.

SCENE 1

*The next morning. Lights up on CAROLITA. She
wears oversized heels meant for an adult. Her
hair flies all over the place, because she is in a
convertible as it travels south along the I-5 freeway
in Washington State.*

CAROLITA
"Andate a la chucha, weon culiao aweonao, concha de
tu madre, voy a sacarte la cresta, hijo de la gran puta
aweonao." You should have heard all the swearing that
went on when Dad found Mom necking with Bill O'Neill
last night. The kind that sounds super hilarious or totally
rude in English. When you translate swearing, it's always
shocking or just plain dumb to people. Like, "Go back
to your mother's cunt, son of a great big whore, fucked--
up-the-ass mother's cunt, I'm going to beat the coxcomb
off you." My mom's Argentinian friend always says, "the
parrot's cunt." Like if she drops something, she doesn't say
"fuck" or "shit." She says, "la concha de la lora." Anyways.
There was a lot of swearing. All us kids were sleeping in
Maria's commune's basement, but me and my friend Tavito
had snuck upstairs to take in the cumbia dancing. My dad
grabbed me and my sister Lupe and threw us in the car.

8

SCENE 2

*Summer 1979. Same day as scene one. Afternoon.
MANUEL, LUPE, and CAROLITA speed through
the desert in a 1964 orange VW convertible. "With
a Little Luck," by Paul McCartney and Wings plays
full blast. CAROLITA and LUPE sit in the back.
Their hair blows in all directions.*

MANUEL

(*whooping at the top of his lungs and then singing along
to the song at the top of his lungs*) There is no end to
what we can do together, there is no end, there is no end!
(*turning the radio down*) Your mother hasn't shaved her
legs in weeks and her shortest armpit hair is an inch long.
She's stopped plucking her eyebrows, giving a whole new
meaning to the term "angry look." Not to mention that she
no longer believes in deodorant, bras, or housework.

CAROLITA

That's 'cuz she's a poet.

LUPE

And a feminist.

CAROLITA

No. A RADICAL feminist.

LUPE

Radical feminists hate men.

MANUEL

(*turning radio off*) My point exactly. Your mother is now a
man-hater.

CAROLITA

She's not a lesbian. She likes Bill.

LUPE

Shut up, you idiot.

CAROLITA

She was kissing Bill on the chesterfield.

MANUEL

She was supposed to be finding herself these last
few weeks.

LUPE

(*to CAROLITA*) What are you, British now? "Chesterfield."

MANUEL

Who knew that "finding herself" included making out
with other men at Maria's so-called commune?

LUPE

(*to CAROLITA*) It's a couch, duh.

CAROLITA

(*giving LUPE the finger*) Fuck you. Sit on this and
spin, bitch.

MANUEL

Hey! If you don't stop in five seconds I WILL slap. Five!

LUPE

That would be a random act of violence –

MANUEL

Four!

LUPE
And you could get in real big trouble with the law.

MANUEL
Three!

CAROLITA
We already ARE in real big trouble with the law, you idiot.

LUPE
No, we're not.

MANUEL
Two and a half!

CAROLITA
Yeah, like, he took us from Mom and we've been driving
for hours with the top down and the radio full blast across
the border and into the U.S., where we've traversed almost
all of Washington State –

LUPE|
"Traversed"?

MANUEL
Two!

CAROLITA
And he's trying to get us back to Chile, where we are
forbidden to enter.

MANUEL
That's all your mother's fault. Due to being a radical who
left you behind to take up arms on the day of the coup
and a hippie who writes terrible poetry and doesn't do her

hair and shows half her ass cheek through the holes in her jeans. Which she hasn't washed in weeks, I might add. You did the right thing, girls, in coming with me.

LUPE
Dad, you were crying at the party, and when you gave us the choice to come with you or stay at Maria's commune with Mom –

CAROLITA
We thought you meant –

CAROLITA and LUPE
Home.

MANUEL
That is what I meant.

CAROLITA
No, Dad, not THAT home –

MANUEL
We only have one home. And your mother can follow if she pleases.

CAROLITA
She doesn't even know where we are –

MANUEL
Or she can stay behind with the hippie.

Lights up on LAURA. She carries a Samsonite and a compass.

LAURA

My beautiful Chile: what does it mean to be a
revolutionary? Manuel and I jumping up and down on the
Alameda the night Allende won, going to the shantytowns
to teach reading and writing as part of the literacy
campaign, joining thousands of others in loading food
at the train station to make sure it was transported after
the truckers' union was bought by the CIA and went on
strike to bring the country to a halt, studying documents
deep into the night detailing the plan to resist the coup
we all knew was coming, learning how to use arms from
a Mapuche leader, until the final victory always, always,
always. Is exile revolutionary? No. But when your name
is on a list, and it's only a matter of days before they find
you and dispose of you, you have to ask, what do you
surrender? Your violent oceans and towering mountains?
Your children? What does it mean to be a mother?

Back to the car.

CAROLITA

Dad, this is a kidnapping, just so you know.

LUPE

No, it isn't.

MANUEL

I'm your father, for God's sake. A kidnapping! Carolita,
you're a little girl. I know this is hard for you to hear, but
your mother left us –

CAROLITA

No –

MANUEL
Remember?

CAROLITA
She left YOU.

LUPE elbows CAROLITA.

We enter LUPE's world. She stands up in the car, holding her purple unicorn stuffy.

LUPE
Months ago, my mom's crying woke me up. And I heard my dad say, "I don't like your poem, Laura, I just don't like it." And she read him another verse about how once an exile, always an exile, and he repeated, "I don't like it. I just don't." And something told me to go to them. So I did, with my purple unicorn stuffy, my first toy in Canada, given to me by the Interfaith church, the one that helps refugees. And they were lying in bed. He had his arms crossed, and her glasses were steamed from the tears. Like the day of the coup in Chile, when we listened to Allende's last speech on the radio and the bombing began, and I didn't know we'd end up on our knees with military guns digging into the backs of our heads.

Beat.

I didn't know we'd end up in Vancouver.

Beat.

It was pouring rain the night I went to them, and there was a clap of thunder, and I was sure it was a bomb. I opened my mouth and screamed. And I dove onto their bed.

14

Back to the world of the car.

LUPE

Dad, what she's trying to say is that I don't think it's allowed to just take your kids away from the mother and leave Canada and stuff and not even tell her or anyone else about it. Like, I think we actually ARE in big trouble with the law now.

CAROLITA

No –

LUPE

Let's just turn around and go back, Dad.

CAROLITA

HE is –

LUPE

It's not too late.

MANUEL

Girls! Your mother left us! I don't know how to say it without breaking your hearts: she's been sitting cross-legged making macramé in Maria's supposed commune for weeks instead of taking care of you.

LUPE

But she still sees us.

CAROLITA

Like, all the time.

MANUEL
    Okay. How to put this? She doesn't believe in the maternal
    instinct. She says it's a patriarchal construct.

CAROLITA
    Oh, yeah, she told me that.

LUPE
    Liar. She told ME.

MANUEL
    I can see her point from a societal point of view, but as a
    scientist who has to revalidate his degree in this fucking
    country, I am telling you that parenting is part of the
    survival instinct, as it is for all species.

LUPE
    She said motherhood is overrated.

MANUEL
    What a wonderful thing to tell your own daughter. We're
    going home. If she doesn't believe in the maternal instinct
    she can stay in the stupid commune. If the maternal
    instinct exists – and it DOES – it will lead her to us.

CAROLITA
    Dad, this isn't a science experiment, like when you take us
    to the UBC lab and show us a picture of a bottle on its side
    and ask us to draw the liquid in it –

MANUEL
    You did such a good job! –

CAROLITA

Or like when you make us watch a passing plane and take note that the sound drifts behind it. Or like when you ask us if time has an ending, then what comes after?

MANUEL

What comes after?

CAROLITA

Or like when you look at your watch and tell us to guess when a minute is over –

MANUEL

(*looking at his watch*) Let's do it right now –

LUPE

(*to CAROLITA, referring to her list*) We get it already!

CAROLITA

This is like life and death, Dad. Totally brutal, like telenovela –

LUPE

You've never even watched a telenovela, you show-off!

CAROLITA

(*giving LUPE the finger*) But it doesn't have to be, Dad. You can just turn the car around, and it can be more like *The Love Boat.*

LUPE

Excuse me while I go puke.

MANUEL

Stupid gringo shows.

CAROLITA starts singing the theme song from
The Love Boat, *à la Jack Jones. After two lines,*
MANUEL joins in. They sing one line together.
Then CAROLITA stops singing, and MANUEL
sings one line alone.

CAROLITA
Without, like, fist fights and kidnappings and getting murdered by men with guns at the final port of call.

LUPE
Dad! You didn't take us because of the commune. You took us because you let your emotions get the better of you when you saw Mom with Bill.

CAROLITA
Love is everywhere, Dad! Like, maybe you'll find someone else –

LUPE elbows CAROLITA.

CAROLITA
Ow!!!

MANUEL
(*holding back tears*) I took you because I'm your father. I take care of you. I put you first. Not some ideology or another lover or some journey that has nothing to do with you. I put you first. And you belong in your rightful home.

Beat.

CAROLITA
How can it be our rightful home if we don't even remember it?

LUPE

I remember Chile.

CAROLITA

Well, when I close my eyes and try to remember, all I see
is black. And I hear, like, fuzz. Like the buzzing sound the
TV makes when it's trying to find a signal.

LUPE

The mud road. The yellow house. The pink rose bush.
The monkey puzzle tree. Our school smocks. Grandma
and Grandpa whispering at the dining-room table during
curfew. The taste of condensed milk. The smell of our
leather school bags.

CAROLITA

Did you always remember, or is it just coming back
to you now?

LUPE

Both.

CAROLITA

All I see is black. No, more like snow. Not SNOW snow,
like snow on the TV screen when it can't find a signal.

LUPE

It's beautiful.

CAROLITA

It's like I look for a channel, turning the dial over and over,
clockwise till infinity, and snow and fuzz and that's it.

LUPE

It's beautiful and ours. You and me in matching outfits, ribbons in our hair and patent-leather shoes. The taste of rosehip jam, the smell of Grandma's yerba mate, a thread of smoke coming from the tip of the volcano in the distance, the sound of my name being called from across the way. Lupe! Lupe! Lupe! Me running towards it, beaming and calling back in the mother tongue. You following.

We enter MANUEL's world. He stands up.

MANUEL

I first saw her on a bench, it was 1965. She was seventeen and in her first year of social work. I was twenty-two and in my last year of metaphysics. We were both in residence at the Technological University in Santiago.

Beat.

We fought the first time we met. I was a social democrat. She was a socialist revolutionary.

Beat.

On our first date we went to a Victor Jara concert.

Beat.

It's due to the careful analysis of my family history and the economic model of our society that I finally saw the light. And I went from social democrat – a reformist – to socialist revolutionary.

The coup happened on September 11, 1973. Pinochet bombed the presidential palace, Allende was killed defending it, and the ultra-right wing fascist dictatorship began. My best friend Lucho was amongst the first to be executed. For being a socialist revolutionary.

Back in the car world, LUPE strategizes about how to make sure the car continues on its journey south. She wants to go to Chile now.

LUPE
(*to MANUEL*) Maria was in bed with Roger. I saw them.

MANUEL
You see?

CAROLITA
(*to LUPE*) You're such a liar.

MANUEL
Bad influences –

CAROLITA
(*to LUPE*) I saw them and told you about it.

MANUEL
All of them.

CAROLITA
(*to LUPE*) You always try to get the glory. Show-off. Exaggerator.

LUPE
(*giving CAROLITA the finger*) I know you are, but what am I?!

CAROLITA
(*giving LUPE the finger*) Fuck you, bitch.

MANUEL
One and a half!

LUPE
Maria was in bed with Roger. Naked. While his wife, the baby-blonde, danced to the reggae show on Co-op Radio in the living room, and Maria's husband was on the tugboats for the week.

MANUEL
This is what I'm trying to explain to you girls. These people, hell, why not just say it, these WOMEN have lost their moral compasses completely. And to top it all off, they're MOTHERS. What kind of mother abandons her family for a commune? Un-fucking-believable.

CAROLITA
She said she needed time to think. To write poetry. To find out what lies between the black and white. And you had to learn how to father and how to mother. That's what she said. How to cook, how to clean, how to care for us properly. And now you know. And you can turn around and tell her. We won't tell her all you know how to make are hot dogs with burned buns. We'll say you fed us cazuelas and pasteles de choclo and humitas and sopaipillas and empanadas and manjar and pastas and casseroles and quiches –

MANUEL
What kind of woman abandons her children?

CAROLITA
   And soufflés and –

LUPE
   Mom says you're a sexist pig 'cuz you see ladies only as
   madonnas or whores.

CAROLITA
   Like Mom would ever say the word "ladies." She would say
   the word "women."

LUPE
   You think you're so fucking smart, you fucking little bitch.

CAROLITA
   Sticks and stones will break my bones –

MANUEL
   Zero!

        MANUEL haphazardly slaps and misses the girls.

LUPE
   Dad! –

CAROLITA
   But names will never hurt me.

LUPE
   (*giving CAROLITA the finger, talking to MANUEL*) Focus
   on the driving.

MANUEL
   And you two focus on the matter at hand.

CAROLITA
What matter?

LUPE
That's for us to know and you to find out.

MANUEL
The matter at hand is that you are both children and you should behave like children. Carolita, you are eleven years old, and Lupe, you are twelve: CHILDREN. Look at the scenery, talk about make-believe, tell each other a story. I don't know.

LUPE
There. I'm looking at the scenery. Oh, there is none! Unless you call being surrounded by long loads and wide loads and endless billboards "scenery."

CAROLITA
I don't see ENDLESS billboards. You're such a liar, always making stuff up.

LUPE
(*reading billboards*) "Cascadia: Home of the Bigfoot Bagel," "Happy Donuts" –

CAROLITA
That's only two!

MANUEL
And for your information, I would say the same thing about your mother and her friends if they were men. And also for your information, Maria's ridiculous commune is off limits to you girls now –

LUPE
Does that mean we get to go with you to your night classes at UBC?

CAROLITA
Of course the commune's off limits! We're leaving North America for, like, ever! (*looking up at the sky*) HELP!

LUPE
Don't tell me you believe in God now.

MANUEL
The place is a pigsty.

LUPE
I was there when Maria said, "I'm going on strike. I will no longer labour in this house for free, which is slavery. And I'm taking back my body. I will no longer let men have control over my means of reproduction."

CAROLITA
You were NOT there! Tavito told us about it –

LUPE
(*covering her ears*) La la la la la!

MANUEL
You mean "means of production."

LUPE
No! "REproduction."

MANUEL
What?!

CAROLITA

Once, when we were over there, I found Mom's bra in
the freezer.

MANUEL

WHAT?!

LUPE

(*to CAROLITA*) Duh, she put it there as a political
statement.

MANUEL

Was the hippie there?

LUPE

No, Dad, this was after they banned all men from the
commune, except on party nights.

MANUEL

I wonder what "political" statement I would be making if I
put my dirty underwear in the meat drawer.

CAROLITA

Roger's wife, the baby-blonde –

MANUEL

Her name is Sharon –

LUPE

Dad! It's Shannon!

MANUEL

Whatever her name is, use it. Don't just call her "Roger's
wife, the baby-blonde" –

CAROLITA
Hello! I was trying to say that whatever her name is, she said the bra in the freezer was like an art installation

MANUEL
I'll tell you what art is, girls: the poems of Neruda, the songs of Violeta Parra. Me taking a shit and putting it on display is not art.

CAROLITA
Dad! You are so filthy and disgusting –

LUPE
What are you? Victorian? It's 1979.

> MANUEL turns on the radio. "New Kid in Town" by the Eagles is playing.

> Beat.

> CAROLITA sighs.

CAROLITA
PLEASE, Dad, can we turn around and go home now? PLEASE. 'Cuz if you're trying to scare the shit out of Mom to prove a point, I think she prolly already got it.

MANUEL
We ARE going home. (pointing to the sky in front of them) Look at that cloud formation! Just like a condor!

LUPE
It's a sign!

CAROLITA
We don't even have any suitcases! Plus we always have to PUSH our car, we'll never make it!

MANUEL
Keep your eyes peeled for the Golden Arches, girls. It's dinner time.

MANUEL turns up the volume and whoops.
He sings along to "New Kid in Town." MANUEL
hums along to the song until the end of the scene.

LUPE
(*to CAROLITA*) She'll find us.

CAROLITA
'Cuz the maternal instinct will lead her to us?

LUPE
I don't know.

CAROLITA
What if the maternal instinct DOESN'T exist?

LUPE
She's on her way, I can feel it.

CAROLITA
And then what?

LUPE
We'll all be together.

CAROLITA
Where?

LUPE

    I don't know.

CAROLITA

    Where do YOU want to go?

LUPE

    The smell of the mud, the scent of the pink rosebush, my
    best friend Nati singing my name. You learning how to
    ride a bike.

CAROLITA

    I don't remember.

LUPE

    Dos en Uno bubblegum melting in your mouth?

CAROLITA

    No. But I do remember the metallic taste of fear on
    my tongue.

    "New Kid in Town" morphs into the sound of wind.

SCENE 3

The convertible travels south in 1979. On a different part of the stage, the wind blows on a big black plastic garbage bag caught in barbed wire in the Arizona desert in 2020. On a third part of the stage, ARCANGEL, a twenty-year-old man, arms outstretched like Christ as he rides on top of a train in northern Mexico, is whipped by the wind. He is in 2020.

ARCANGEL raps, accompanied by an original musical composition.

ARCANGEL
 This song is about a wetback
 I get called a wetback
"Evil" and "illegal,"
 Funny – they get called an "ex-pat"

 I get called a wetback
 Literally slippery
 Wet from the river
 That still makes me shivery

 Got this backpack
 Like Dora
 But they don't find me aDORAble
 Also an explorah
 But they find my kind deplorable
 Exploitable, deportable
 Hope they don't find me ...
 At all

See they call us wetbacks
Why? 'Cuz of the river
That the gringos call Grande
The one we call Bravo
This beach is the opposite of Cabo!
This is the crossroads
Where we cross slow
Because the cops and patrols
Stay watchful

Callin' me a wetback
Though my back is dry
From the wind
From the sun
Heaven's merciless sky
Face covered by a shirt
To keep the dirt from my eyes
Through the dust storms
Curse this whole earth
I despise

Body wrapped in a bag
The opposite of Glad, though
Mad and mad broke
From that close
To dashed hopes

You kick us off this train
And we'll be back at the
Plateau
Just to freeze
Just to risk
A slip
Or the slightest tip
This beast we ride is quick

And it's wild
But I'm on this trip
Seeing shooting star and cars
Meteor showers and flowers
Green valleys and bridges
I'm suspended in the sky

A monarch butterfly whispers
The names of my Elders
And lost brothers and sisters

The beast is always looking for a feast
He eats: the dangling limbs of my kin
While within, my stomach is empty
The beast sees plenty
But I stay on his path, snaking from side to side
Winding my way to where the monarch flies:

El Norte

SCENE 4

The crack of dawn. TEENAGED GIRL, wearing only a huge black plastic garbage bag walks through the Arizona desert in 2020. A helicopter flies low. The sound of a distant bombo criollo playing a malambo rhythm. TEENAGED GIRL ducks under a shrub and finds a plastic water bottle with a note. She looks around and drinks the water.

In Arizona in 1979, the convertible has pulled over. LUPE and MANUEL sleep inside.

CAROLITA walks an imaginary runway in her oversized heels. Her hair flies all over the place.

CAROLITA
(*talking to the audience, referring to her heels*) I found these at the laundromat. They help my flat feet. They create an arch. See? When I wear these, I look like I'm twenty-one. Nobody would ever know I'm really a kid, right?

Beat.

'Kay.

Beat.

I'm gonna tell you a secret: My name is not actually Carolita Gonzalez Torres, it's Carol Gordon Taylor, and I'm gonna marry the Bionic Woman and be a stewardess with Braniff, based in Honolulu. My sister's gonna be a scientist at MIT.

Beat.

'Kay.

Beat.

I'm gonna tell you another secret. Last night when we parked to sleep, I noticed that our car is no longer a fifteen-year-old orange Volkswagen Beetle convertible with the trunk held down by a coat hanger. It's now a brand new, hot pink Cadillac convertible like Malibu Barbie drives. All stretched out, all chrome and shit. But my dad and Lupe can't seem to tell. I don't know when it happened. I don't know HOW it happened, but it did.

CAROLITA breaks into a few lines of the "Car Wash" disco song and dances.

> *YOUNG MAN WITH GUNS appears. He is in 2020.*

YOUNG MAN WITH GUNS
Hands up! Migra!

CAROLITA
Help!

YOUNG MAN WITH GUNS
Ain't no one gonna help you but me, señorita.

CAROLITA
(*towards the car*) Papi!

34

YOUNG MAN WITH GUNS
You are in America now. And we're gonna send you right
back to Chihuahua.

CAROLITA
The dog?

YOUNG MAN WITH GUNS
The place. (*speaking with a very heavy American accent*)
¿Dónde están sus mamas and papas?

CAROLITA
I speak English. And I'm not Chihuahuean. I'm Chilean.
And this is great. Just great. I'm only eleven, and this is the
second time men with guns point them at my head. They
raided our house when I was four and dragged me into
the yard and held guns to my head. Not that I remember.
(*looking up at the sky, referring to this being the second time
guns are pointed to her head*) Thanks, God!

YOUNG MAN WITH GUNS
(*still pointing his gun*) Keep your hands up. You walked all
the way from Chilly to Arizona?

CAROLITA
Of course not. We took taxis and planes and buses
and stuff –

YOUNG MAN WITH GUNS
Hands UP!

CAROLITA
My dad and my sister are sleeping in our car over there.
We're going back to Chile.

YOUNG MAN WITH GUNS
You're on your way TO Mexico?

CAROLITA
Newsflash: Chile's not in Mexico. It's way down South.

YOUNG MAN WITH GUNS
(*lowering his gun and starting to walk away*) If you're
heading south, I guess that's not our concern.

CAROLITA
(*lowering her arms*) You keep saying "we," but there's only
one of you.

YOUNG MAN WITH GUNS
The others are on their way. And they might just shoot first
and ask questions later.

CAROLITA
Can you go tell my dad he has to go back to Canada? We
left there three days ago already! Tell him you're gonna
arrest him for kidnapping –

YOUNG MAN WITH GUNS
(*reaching for one of his guns and for his walkie-talkie*) He
kidnapped somebody?

CAROLITA
Hello! Yes! Me and my sister. He's taking us back to Chile,
'cuz he hates North America.

YOUNG MAN WITH GUNS
Why?

CAROLITA
The people. The coldness of the people. The life. Or lack thereof. That's what he says all the time. He looks around and shouts: "Where is the LIFE? Where? WHERE, goddammit?!"

WALKIE-TALKIE
Angel Number Four: Have you found some wetbacks? What are your coordinates? We're coming to offer backup. Over.

    Beat.

CAROLITA
You're an angel?

YOUNG MAN WITH GUNS
A guardian angel, serving my country.

CAROLITA
I thought angels were happy.

    YOUNG MAN WITH GUNS starts to walk away.

    At the car, LUPE tosses and turns in her sleep, the sound of the walkie-talkie reaching her dreams.

LUPE
(*standing on the car seat, holding her purple unicorn stuffy*)
There's a water stain on the ceiling right above my bed in the shape of Chile. I fix my eyes on it in the dark when I hear my mother cry at night. A distant sound wakes me, and I reach for that Chile stain, but all I see is open sky, and I fall asleep again.

LUPE sits back on her seat, still asleep.

CAROLITA
(*calling to YOUNG MAN WITH GUNS as he walks away*) Sad guardian angel, lend me your guns and baseball cap, and I'll pretend I'm you and scare the shit out of my dad. I know how to look twenty-one. I know how to flee and make it look like I'm only on a Sunday stroll, I know how to make myself invisible in a hostile place. I can pull this off.

WALKIE-TALKIE
Hello? Angel Number Four? Have you found some lettuce pickers? Over.

YOUNG MAN WITH GUNS
(*into the walkie-talkie*) Still looking. Over.

WALKIE-TALKIE
Roger that. Over and out.

At the shrub, TEENAGED GIRL hears the helicopter get farther away. The malambo bombo gets louder, closer.

TEENAGED GIRL
(*after sipping some water*) Thank you, Yemaya, or Oshun, or the armadillo that just scared the fuck out of me, for the miracle of water. Thank you. I have stood looking up at the sky, mouth wide open, praying for a cloud to come along and piss some rain into the gaping hole of my existence, but a plastic water bottle will do just fine. Thank you. The fucking coyote took my water, my money, and my clothes. After he raped me and left me for dead, floating face up in the river, my womb shrivelled into a prune. The current

took me, and my baby retreated into my pelvic bone, the fluttering of butterfly wings gone forever. The Big Dipper twinkled like a string of Christmas lights in the black sky, and I let out the howl of a wolf until its ladle scooped me out and laid me face down on the shore. The life growing inside me died, but I lived.

TEENAGED GIRL has more water.

I know I have asked a lot of you already, Ancestors-That-Are-Always-with-Me, but I need you to make sure the migra don't come any closer. Here's an offering to our Mother Earth.

TEENAGED GIRL pours some of the water on the earth.

WALKIE-TALKIE
Hello? Angel Number Four? Give us an update. Over.

CAROLITA
Aren't you gonna answer that?

YOUNG MAN WITH GUNS
In a moment. (*pulling out one of his guns*) This one's range of fire is a hundred and sixty feet. Ready to hold it?

CAROLITA
Duh.

YOUNG MAN WITH GUNS
(*clicking the safety on*) Safety's on.

CAROLITA studies it for a while and then poses like Charlie's Angels while humming the Charlie's Angels *theme song. Then she loses interest in it.*

CAROLITA
What's that one?

YOUNG MAN WITH GUNS
G36. A little more old-fashioned. Real pretty.

CAROLITA
That's the first time I hear "pretty" to describe a gun.

YOUNG MAN WITH GUNS
You wanna feel good about looking at your weapons, 'cuz they create a sight that can never be unseen.

WALKIE-TALKIE
Report on your patrol status, Angel Number Four! Over and out.

YOUNG MAN WITH GUNS
(*to WALKIE-TALKIE, though not into the walkie-talkie*) Chillax. (*back to CAROLITA*) Though feelings should never factor into the equation. They can get the best of you, and that pretty much always leads to no good.

CAROLITA sings "You're No Good" à la Linda Ronstadt.

YOUNG MAN WITH GUNS
What the –

CAROLITA keeps singing "You're No Good."

YOUNG MAN WITH GUNS
Okay then. Give me back the gun and walk away.

CAROLITA stares at him, keeping the gun.
A standoff.

At the shrub, the helicopter is almost gone.

MANUEL tosses and turns in his sleep. He stands
up in the car, dreaming.

LAURA, wearing a suede miniskirt and patent-
leather go-go boots, appears. She is outside her
university residence in Santiago. MANUEL is
standing and looking up at her. It is a warm
spring night in 1965. LAURA is scaling down
the wall of the building with a bunch of knotted
sheets. LAURA's UNIVERSITY RESIDENCE
GIGGLING FRIEND is at the window, keeping
a look out. Both of them are laughing hysterically,
trying to keep the volume down. MANUEL is
hanging on to the bottom of the sheets as he waits
on the ground.

LAURA
(*through her laughter, in a loud whisper*) Violeta Parra,
here I come!

MANUEL sings Victor Jara's "A Cochabamba me
voy" in a loud whisper through his laughter, dancing
on the spot.

LAURA
(*through her laughter, in a loud whisper*) Fuck!

> MANUEL *continues singing in a loud whisper*
> *and dancing.*

LAURA
(*laughing and in a loud whisper*) Fuck!

> MANUEL *sings one more line of "A Cochabamba*
> *me voy," still dancing, and then stops singing.*

MANUEL
(*in a loud whisper*) Are you peeing yourself?!

LAURA
(*laughing uncontrollably and in a loud whisper*) Yes!

> MANUEL *doubles over laughing. LAURA's*
> *UNIVERSITY RESIDENCE GIGGLING*
> *FRIEND laughs harder, mouth covered.*

LAURA
(*to LAURA's UNIVERSITY RESIDENCE GIGGLING*
FRIEND, in a loud whisper) Grab me a pair of dry
underwear!

> *LAURA's UNIVERSITY RESIDENCE*
> *GIGGLING FRIEND disappears. LAURA*
> *finally reaches the ground. She can't stop laughing,*
> *alongside MANUEL. LAURA's UNIVERSITY*
> *RESIDENCE GIGGLING FRIEND reappears,*
> *throws down a pair of dry underwear, and*
> *disappears. LAURA catches the underwear.*

MANUEL
(*not skipping a beat, pulling out his handkerchief, and*
wiping the pee off LAURA's bare legs) We'll catch the tail

end of Violeta Parra, but Victor Jara's full set. I have enough money for one empanada and one pisco sour. We can share. Lucho's holding a spot for us at his table. Neruda's dropping by tonight, too. (*finishing up the wiping of the pee*) There. (*singing "A Cochabamba me voy" and dancing again*)

LAURA
Turn around.

> MANUEL *does so and keeps singing as* LAURA *takes off her wet underwear, throws them into a bush, and puts on the dry ones.*

> MANUEL *sings a line of "A Cochabamba me voy" and dances.*

LAURA
Let's go.

> MANUEL *sings the next line.*

> LAURA *and* MANUEL *sing the following line of "A Cochabamba me voy" together. They run off laughing, hand in hand.*

MANUEL
(*back in the car, in a dream state*) Lucho! Lucho! What would you say to me now? That this is criminal? That I should turn around and go back with my girls and work things out with her? Or am I at the point of no return? Lucho, you who gave your life to the cause, tell me, is it exile or a broken heart that led me to this?

> MANUEL *sits back down and continues sleeping.*

43

SCENE 5

GENERAL JUANA AZURDUY DE PADILLA,
riding a horse and holding an 1850s gun, arrives at
the shrub in 2020. CAROLITA witnesses the scene.

TEENAGED GIRL
(*looking around*) I smell jasmine.

GENERAL JUANA AZURDUY DE PADILLA
Each ghost announces its arrival with a particular scent.
Although I would say that I am more of an apparition. No,
actually I'm a statue. A monument. So you should only be
smelling marble. Although who knows if marble smells
like anything at all –

TEENAGED GIRL
My nostrils are flaring with the scent of jasmine.

GENERAL JUANA AZURDUY DE PADILLA
That must mean you really need me. And my gun.

TEENAGED GIRL
I do. And I really needed it when they caught me trying to
unionize the Disney assembly plant just south of the wall
here. I was forced to flee.

GENERAL JUANA AZURDUY DE PADILLA
Into the heart of the empire?!

TEENAGED GIRL
Please help me.

GENERAL JUANA AZURDUY DE PADILLA
(*passing her the gun*) You needed this then, you need it
now, and in the immediate future.

TEENAGED GIRL
(*referring to GENERAL JUANA AZURDUY DE
PADILLA's wardrobe*) Loving the uniform.

GENERAL JUANA AZURDUY DE PADILLA
Can't say the same for your attire.

TEENAGED GIRL
I recognize you from my independent studies. You are
General Juana Azurduy de Padilla, born in 1780 in the
Altiplano, half Indian, half Spanish, like the rest of us. You
fought for our independence from the Spaniards on the
front lines with your army of two hundred women, in over
a hundred skirmishes, two centuries ago, while pregnant,
in what is now Bolivia and Argentina. (*to Mother Earth*)
Thank you, Pachamama, for sending her to me.

GENERAL JUANA AZURDUY DE PADILLA
And you've kept up the struggle.

TEENAGED GIRL
Yes.

GENERAL JUANA AZURDUY DE PADILLA
It's why I've come.

TEENAGED GIRL
The cost is high. Is it worth it?

GENERAL JUANA AZURDUY DE PADILLA
You are the only one who can answer that, sister. I lost my
compañero and four children to the struggle –

TEENAGED GIRL
Your husband was beheaded, your children died of fevers
during the wars –

GENERAL JUANA AZURDUY DE PADILLA
Except for my beloved Luisa ... you've lost your home and
your clothes – even your underpants! – but you don't need
to lose the girl that grows inside you.

TEENAGED GIRL
She's gone, a dead weight in my womb now, looking for a
place to drop. I always dreamt of a girl. Apple cheeks and
jet-black hair.

GENERAL JUANA AZURDUY DE PADILLA
She's alive.

TEENAGED GIRL
No. Frida just came to me, with that gaping hole in her
centre. I took it as a sign. Adelita, too, from the Mexican
Revolution, and Comandanta Ramona of the Zapatistas,
Comandante Celia of the Cuban Revolution, and
Comandante Ana María of the Salvadoran one –

GENERAL JUANA AZURDUY DE PADILLA
(*looking around, pleased*) This desert is populated!

TEENAGED GIRL
I ask each of you: Is the cost worth it?

GENERAL JUANA AZURDUY DE PADILLA
What did my compañeras say?

TEENAGED GIRL
Variations on what you just said. Plus that only history will
tell. And yes. Some said yes.

GENERAL JUANA AZURDUY DE PADILLA
(*looking around and yelling*) Where are you, sisters in the
struggle?!

TEENAGED GIRL
Shhh!!!

GENERAL JUANA AZURDUY DE PADILLA
(*still yelling*) Come out, come out wherever you are!

TEENAGED GIRL
Shhhh!!!

GENERAL JUANA AZURDUY DE PADILLA
(*still yelling*) Let's have a consciousness-raising meeting,
compañeras! (*to TEENAGED GIRL*) Middle-class gringas
call those "book clubs" now.

TEENAGED GIRL
SHHH!!! (*whispering*) You'll attract the fucking
migra – or worse, the white-supremacist vigilantes. The
revolucionarias came to me in Sonora, just south of the
border here, in my terrifying nights, when I was sure the
wind rattling the tin door of my house was the Disney
rent-a-cops, come to get me after the bosses found out
I was the one who organized the strike at the plant
demanding to be paid more than fifty bucks a week.
They came to dispose of me in a bag (*referring to the bag*

47

she's wearing) like this one when their job was done. We were assembling talking Kermit piggy banks, super cute by the way.

GENERAL JUANA AZURDUY DE PADILLA
Are the Disney rent-a-cops the ones that took your underpants?

TEENAGED GIRL
No, that's a different story –

GENERAL JUANA AZURDUY DE PADILLA
So you got away from the rent-a-cops? Forgive me if I don't know all the details, I was too busy getting a kick out of watching the gringas burn their bras on Fifth Avenue.

TEENAGED GIRL
Now, in 1996? I thought that only happened in the sixties.

GENERAL JUANA AZURDUY DE PADILLA
I live outside of human time now. All eras are happening simultaneously for me.

TEENAGED GIRL
Fascinating.

GENERAL JUANA AZURDUY DE PADILLA
Psychedelic!

TEENAGED GIRL
I got away from the rent-a-cops, but I belong back South.

GENERAL JUANA AZURDUY DE PADILLA
Then you already know the answer to the question.

TEENAGED GIRL sighs.

TEENAGED GIRL
But what is going to happen, Juana? What are we
going to do?

GENERAL JUANA AZURDUY DE PADILLA
Who knows?! What is going to happen and what you're
going to do doesn't matter as much as what's happenING
and what you're doING. What do you want your daughter
to know about you? That you dropped your head and took
it or that you fought?

TEENAGED GIRL
I lost her crossing the river, along with everything else.

GENERAL JUANA AZURDUY DE PADILLA
She's alive. Take my gun, aim it well at the heart of the
enemy, shoot, and sing (*singing and teaching Amparo
Ochoa's song "Mujer"*) "¡Mujer, semilla fruto, flor, camino!"

TEENAGED GIRL
(*singing*) "¡Mujer, semilla fruto, flor, camino!"

GENERAL JUANA AZURDUY DE PADILLA
(*singing and teaching*) "¡Luchar es altamente femenino!"

TEENAGED GIRL
(*singing*) "¡Luchar es altamente femenino!"

GENERAL JUANA AZURDUY DE PADILLA
There are more shrines of water along the way. Some have
shoes. You are not far from a road. If you follow it, it will
lead you to places that will help, run by others who have

made the journey and their gringo allies. Or shall we call
them compañeros?

TEENAGED GIRL
Sure. And you, Juana? You don't need your gun?

GENERAL JUANA AZURDUY DE PADILLA
Actually, take my horse, too. I just stole it from some of
those white-supremacist-mass-murderer vigilantes while
they destroyed a shrine, dumping out the water, pissing
inside the shoes. And take my uniform. Take it all. Give
me the bag.

TEENAGED GIRL
But what about you?

GENERAL JUANA AZURDUY DE PADILLA
I am the spirit of Juana on my way to Antofagasta, to
breathe life into the statue being erected in my honour in
2020, where the toppled Columbus once stood. I can get
there on the wings of the eagle and the condor. By the way,
be sure to have a ranchero burger. Hot and habit forming.
That's what the freeway billboard I just passed says.

SCENE 6

CAROLITA

(*examining the gun she's holding, referring to the ones on YOUNG MAN WITH GUNS*) These guns are from the future, aren't they?

YOUNG MAN WITH GUNS

There is no future. Only the eternal now.

CAROLITA

They're not from the 1970s.

YOUNG MAN WITH GUNS

You're confused. It's 2020.

CAROLITA

Two zero two zero?!! This all might have to do with the space-time continuum my dad talks about.

WALKIE-TALKIE

Angel Number Four! We've lost one of our horses, but we're on our way! Over and out.

> *TEENAGED GIRL and GENERAL JUANA AZURDUY DE PADILLA can hear the walkie-talkie as they exchange clothes.*

YOUNG MAN WITH GUNS

You really have to go now.

WALKIE-TALKIE

Angel Number Four, we're praying to the Almighty that you're still alive. That some bad hombres from one of

those shithole countries haven't gotten you. God bless you.
God bless America. Over and out.

YOUNG MAN WITH GUNS
(*into his walkie-talkie*) All clear. I'll come to you in a
moment. Over.

WALKIE-TALKIE
Roger that. Over and out.

YOUNG MAN WITH GUNS
(*to CAROLITA*) Give me back my gun.

CAROLITA
(*keeping the gun*) Hold on a sec, sad angel. I told my dad
I knew about the magnetic north, and he got super happy
since he's a metaphysicist – well, he WAS a metaphysicist,
he's actually a janitor now. So's my mom. Anyways. I
told him I knew about the magnetic north so he would
understand that if it's magnetic, that's why we're in the
North, because the magnet pulled us here, away from the
South. And you know what he said?

YOUNG MAN WITH GUNS
No.

CAROLITA
That the sun had just flipped upside down and that that
only happens once every eleven years and that it had just
flipped ON my eleventh birthday and so now the magnet
was South. Not North. But South. Do you understand?

YOUNG MAN WITH GUNS
No.

CAROLITA starts crying.

YOUNG MAN WITH GUNS
What's wrong?

CAROLITA
Why do I have to be a poor Latina girl in the North, why?

YOUNG MAN WITH GUNS
Why do I have to be on the border?

YOUNG MAN WITH GUNS starts crying.

CAROLITA
Are you crying, too?

YOUNG MAN WITH GUNS
(*nodding*) This is the first time I've cried.

CAROLITA
In your life?!

YOUNG MAN WITH GUNS
Since my first kill. When I was eleven, like you. The only time my uncle ever touched me was to put his palm over the top of my hand, when he showed me how to pull the trigger. I've never been touched again. By anybody.

CAROLITA
I am not eleven. I am twenty-one.

YOUNG MAN WITH GUNS
No. I am twenty-one.

CAROLITA
There is a kind of pain, a kind of knowing ... you are the
master of your own life when you are twenty-one.

They cry together.

*Back at the shrub, TEENAGED GIRL has finished
putting on GENERAL JUANA AZURDUY
DE PADILLA's uniform. GENERAL JUANA
AZURDUY DE PADILLA is gone. TEENAGED
GIRL mounts the horse and brandishes the gun.*

TEENAGED GIRL
General Juana Azurduy de Padilla, Pachamama,
Guadalupe, Frida, Bartolina, Adelita, T-Boz, Left Eye,
Chilli, and Princess Leia! I'm calling on you to knock
down every wall. And if I happen to be swallowed into the
bubble of the North, let me be guilt-free and shameless,
like Mariah Carey, that first-generation woman of colour
who came from nothing, brandishing only a cassette tape.
Let me be the Queen she is. Because she understands that
if you're going to be a brown-girl diva, then fucking throw
down and COMMIT. Wherever we fight, whatever wall
we topple, let me COMMIT with no shame whatsoever.
(*rubbing her belly and looking down at it*) You lead the
way, girl.

*TEENAGED GIRL gallops off into the rising sun.
The sound of the malambo bombo, with the sound
of the galloping horse and Aretha Franklin singing
"Respect."*

*YOUNG MAN WITH GUNS and CAROLITA
wail it all out. Like two babies facing each other,
they egg each other on with their crying. It's operatic.*

There's a rhythm to it. Just when you think it's over,
it starts up again.

At the car, LUPE tosses and turns in her sleep again,
the wailing reaching her dreams.

LUPE
(*standing on the car seat in a dream state, holding her*
purple unicorn stuffy) When my mother's crying fades
into a whimper and my eyes have traced the stain I know
by heart from the Atacama to Patagonia, I close my eyes
and have the dream. In it I wear a kilt. And I stand in the
Cascadian temperate rainforest in the middle of a storm
and I dance. Not a highland jig. But a Brazilian batucada.
Like this.

She dances. The wailing continues, the Aretha
Franklin, the malambo, the galloping as well. Now a
batucada comes in.

LUPE
I am surrounded by the sound of hundreds of batucada
drummers and I can't stop dancing. And I am all alone in
this kilt in the North dancing a dance I've never danced
before. But it overtakes my limbs and core and none of
it makes any sense and I know what this dream is trying
to capture, it's the two poles pulling me apart, like the
horses the Spaniards used to tear Túpac Amaru, the Inca
leader who resisted them, limb from limb. I am Túpac.
And I am also the equator, dancing as the planet spins
around the sun.

All the sounds reach a crescendo, as does LUPE's
dancing. It all stops abruptly. LUPE sits back on her
seat, still asleep.

YOUNG MAN WITH GUNS and CAROLITA
stare at each other, worn out from their wailing.
CAROLITA still holds his gun.

GENERAL JUANA AZURDUY DE PADILLA
walks by wearing nothing but the garbage bag.
CAROLITA smells her. YOUNG MAN WITH
GUNS doesn't.

GENERAL JUANA AZURDUY DE PADILLA
(*to CAROLITA*) He's killed men, women, and children.

GENERAL JUANA AZURDUY DE PADILLA
keeps walking.

CAROLITA
Do you smell jasmine?

YOUNG MAN WITH GUNS
Jasmine?

CAROLITA
Yeah, like all of a sudden someone swung a jasmine branch
right under your nose.

YOUNG MAN WITH GUNS
How long has it been since you've hydrated?

On another part of the stage, LAURA, in 1979, runs,
Samsonite in her right hand, compass in her left. She
stops for a rest.

LAURA
Mother, I've been lying to you in my letters to Chile.
Things are not okay. I know you imagined me with him

56

until the day I die, raising my girls in the far South. You did not envision me leaving my girls behind, in a dirty white-stucco house surrounded by ferns, with a man who can only cook a pot of burnt rice, while I sit on a beanbag in a commune of barefoot women.

Beat.

(*looking around*) Where are you, my girls? Where are you?

> *GENERAL JUANA AZURDUY DE PADILLA passes her. LAURA smells the air, looks around.*

GENERAL JUANA AZURDUY DE PADILLA
Keep going, compañera, you'll get there soon.

> *LAURA looks around, nods, and keeps running. The walkie-talkie sputters. LAURA hears it.*

YOUNG MAN WITH GUNS
My uncle will be here any minute.

> *CAROLITA puts down the gun, looks at YOUNG MAN WITH GUNS, who goes into a kind of hypnotic state, and walks away. During the next two scenes, YOUNG MAN WITH GUNS ritualistically puts down all of his guns and sets them in a circle around himself.*

> *CAROLITA passes MONARCH BUTTERFLY.*

MONARCH BUTTERFLY
(*singing*) Carolita! Carolita! Carolita!

CAROLITA
(*talking directly to MONARCH BUTTERFLY*) There's a
picture from Chile of me on a tricycle with my best friend
Jimena on the back. But I don't remember her. Is that you,
Jimena, singing my name from across the way?

MONARCH BUTTERFLY
No, it's your great-aunt Lili, banished from the family
home decades ago when I was fourteen for being pregnant.

CAROLITA
For having no control over your means of reproduction?

MONARCH BUTTERFLY
Something like that.

CAROLITA
What are you doing here?

MONARCH BUTTERFLY
(*caressing CAROLITA's face*) Singing your name. If you
ever need anything, sing my name.

> *MONARCH BUTTERFLY continues on her way.*
> *CAROLITA watches her.*

> *Psychedelic, futuristic music plays.*
> *MANUEL dreams in the car.*

MANUEL
(*standing up in the car seat, in a dream state*) Someday,
in the future, there will be these things called "cellular
phones," and I will be able to call you, and you will be able
to call me and ask me to return. You'll get on your knees,
on this "cellphone," and I will be able to see you, because

it will have a built-in video system, and you will beg me to come back, to make you pee your pants with laughter, like on our first date. To make you howl at the moon when I touched your tender spot. You'll hold the "cellphone" up so that it catches your best angle, accentuating your cheekbones, deleting that double chin, bringing out your brown almond eyes, set a little too close together, like a Muppet. I've never told you that. You look like a Muppet. You will have a thing called a "global positioning system." GPS. Which is like a living, breathing map, and it will say you are here and he is there and it will lead you directly to me. And when you find me you will lie prostrate on the floor in front of me. You will crucify yourself, and you will say, "Yes, yes, yes, I am here. Now and forever. Now and forever I am here. And I will never be an exile because I understand that home is YOU. Where you are, I am, and you are home. And that is how we abolish the state. The state of exile."

MANUEL wakes up, looks behind him, and sees LUPE sleeping, but no CAROLITA.

MANUEL

Motherfucking Christ. Carolita!!! (*to himself, getting out of the car*) Goddammit, I'm a terrible father. Lucho, what have I done?! (*wanting to leave the side of the car in order to look for CAROLITA, but not wanting to leave LUPE alone, so staying by the car and calling out*) Carolita!

CAROLITA

(*arriving at the car*) Chillax, Dad.

MANUEL takes CAROLITA in his arms and hugs her desperately.

MANUEL
    My baby girl, my baby girl, don't ever leave like that again.

CAROLITA
    I was just going pee, Dad.

MANUEL
    (*still squeezing her*) Never leave like that again.

LUPE
    (*awake now*) That one's always trying to run away. Ha! As
    if you can flee from the state of exile.

        MANUEL and CAROLITA get in the car.

MANUEL
    Girls, I love you like only a father ever could. Everything
    I'm doing is because I love you like no one else ever will.

CAROLITA and LUPE
    Okay, Dad.

MANUEL
    Let's find a McDonald's.

LUPE
    Again?!

MANUEL
    Yes.

CAROLITA
    Can I get TWO Egg McMuffins?

MANUEL
Yes.

LUPE
Can I get TWO Happy Meals?

MANUEL
Yes.

LUPE and CAROLITA do an elaborate high-five. They drive.

SCENE 7

LAURA, in 1979, waves the compass around and looks at it as she smells the air. The MONARCH BUTTERFLY appears.

MONARCH BUTTERFLY
What's with the liberal feminism?

LAURA
No time for philosophizing, winged sister. I'm trying to retrieve my daughters, abducted by the patriarchy.

MONARCH BUTTERFLY
You've assumed I'm female.

LAURA
What?

MONARCH BUTTERFLY
You called me a sister.

LAURA
Well, I suppose I view butterflies as feminine –

MONARCH BUTTERFLY
Look who's sexist now.

LAURA
What's wrong with being female?

MONARCH BUTTERFLY
Don't you know who I am?

LAURA

You're a monarch butterfly. You fly north when it gets cold
in the South and south when the North goes into deep-
freeze – wait a minute. Why is a butterfly talking? And, more
importantly, why am I engaging? Oh, fuck. Where am I?
Have I been abducted into a Disney movie? Because, let's
make one thing clear: I am a dialectical materialist. I do
not believe in talking animals. I repeat: I do not believe in
talking animals.

MONARCH BUTTERFLY

I do not identify as an animal, but rather as an insect. And
I am the spirit of your aunt Lili.

LAURA

Lili?

MONARCH BUTTERFLY

The one you never met. The one who was beaten and
banished by your grandfather.

LAURA

You mean reincarnation EXISTS?

MONARCH BUTTERFLY

Call it what you want –

LAURA

I mean, I can almost believe in ghosts because of Uncle
Mario's spectre coming to Manuel and me when we found
out I was pregnant with Lupe –

MONARCH BUTTERFLY

Niece! A billboard I just passed said to call "855-We Trust" for
evidence that God exists. Talk to THEM about this stuff.

Beat.

I used to be a ghost in a woman's body; now I am a ghost in a butterfly body. I asked to not come back as a woman, because there is no place on Earth where a woman can walk free of fear. Taking to a dirt road or a ten-lane freeway in the middle of the night, naked, wearing a crown of flowers or diamonds, just dancing and singing on her own under the stars without fear. Nowhere on this pitiful planet. So I said to the universe, don't bring me back as a woman. Bring me back as a winged creature. The point is that I am the spirit of Aunt Lili, whose birth certificate was burned –

LAURA
In the bonfire of your clothes and photographs.

MONARCH BUTTERFLY
I walked all the way north from Chuquicamata to Arequipa, Peru. I lost my child, but I had others. I organized the neighbourhood women. We started a clinic and performed underground abortions.

LAURA
What year was this?

MONARCH BUTTERFLY
1926.

LAURA
What are you doing here?

MONARCH BUTTERFLY
You are the only one from our lineage to ever leave the South behind. I'm here to witness your journey and to offer support. From one exile to another.

LAURA
I'm dying, Aunt Lili.

MONARCH BUTTERFLY
From the state of exile?

LAURA
That too. From this desert with no water in sight.

MONARCH BUTTERFLY
Now, THAT is life and death. Bourgeois pickles like
(*breaks into a blues*) "should I wear deodorant should I
wear a bra should I shave should I wash should I say lady
or woman or girl should I scrub the floor or live like a pig"
(*back to normal speech*) are just, well, bourgeois.

MONARCH BUTTERFLY starts to exit.

LAURA
Where are you going?!

MONARCH BUTTERFLY
North.

LAURA
(*breaking into tears*) Don't go, Aunt Lili, protect me –

MONARCH BUTTERFLY
Since I'm in a butterfly body, I can't protect you. Also, I
need to go north, as butterflies do at this time of year. If
I don't, I'll die, and this time I want to die old, of natural
causes, not young, of an exploding head.

*MONARCH BUTTERFLY keeps leaving, singing
the blues.*

65

(*singing*) "Sister, you'll never get away from your state of exile, longing for pre-exile, praying for post-exile, you'll never be free, oh, hear what I say, you'll never be free, oh, listen to me, niece, you'll always be chained to exile."

LAURA
(*opening her suitcase and pulling out her notebook*) I'm writing this down in my book of poetry. I'm calling it "Compass" and I'll dedicate it to you. Your head exploded, Aunt Lili?

MONARCH BUTTERFLY
The beating at fourteen took its toll. At twenty-four an artery burst and my brain flooded with blood.

MONARCH BUTTERFLY exits.

LAURA
(*to the earth*) I think I just had a spiritual experience, Pachamama.

LAURA puts the notebook back in the suitcase and shakes the compass, humming the blues.

MONARCH BUTTERFLY
(*offstage*) I am flying north. South is in the opposite direction.

SCENE 8

TEENAGED GIRL, in 2020, gallops by on her horse, brandishing her gun.

YOUNG MAN WITH GUNS stands in his circle of his guns.

TEENAGED GIRL
Holy fuck! You're not the migra, you're one of those white-supremacist vigilantes.

UNCLE arrives on foot.

UNCLE
(*aiming a gun at TEENAGED GIRL*) Hands up! Migra! (*to YOUNG MAN WITH GUNS*) What the heck are you doing?! (*to TEENAGED GIRL*) I said hands up! Migra! And give me back my horse!

UNCLE cocks his gun and prepares to shoot. TEENAGED GIRL shoots UNCLE dead. YOUNG MAN WITH GUNS comes out of his spell, cocks his gun, and prepares to shoot TEENAGED GIRL. TEENAGED GIRL shoots YOUNG MAN WITH GUNS dead.

TEENAGED GIRL
Aim well at the heart of the enemy, shoot, and sing.

TEENAGED GIRL dismounts and sings the Amparo Ochoa version of the song "Mujer" while she takes all the guns and closes they eyes of both the dead men.

"Mujer, semilla fruto, flor, camino, luchar es altamente femenino." (*doubling over, feeling her belly*) Juana-Luisa, you deliver quite the kick.

TEENAGED GIRL gallops off with all the guns.

LAURA walks through the desert. She passes the YOUNG MAN WITH GUNS' and UNCLE's ghosts.

SCENE 9

*Later that morning, in 1979. LUPE sits in the front
seat with MANUEL, her hair flying in all directions.
They drive at top speed. "Star Wars Theme /
Cantina Band" by Meco plays on the radio full blast.
MANUEL and LUPE whoop. CAROLITA sits in
the back seat, dry puke on her T-shirt, in a terrible
mood. She pulls out her notebook and starts writing
in it. She writes something on each page, tears the
page out, and throws it in the air. Eventually, there
are pieces of paper swirling all around them, like a
swarm of flies.*

CAROLITA
 I'm writing the names of all the sexist, racist, right-wing
 pigs on these papers!!!

MANUEL
 Keep taking breaths, Carolita! Deep breaths and focus
 on the horizon. You'll feel better soon. (*to LUPE*) Warm
 wind! Yes! WARM wind! Vast turquoise sky! Endless
 horizons in orange hues! It's like the Atacama! Only uglier!

CAROLITA
 (*reading from a piece of paper*) Henry Kissinger! (*throwing
 the piece of paper*) You're a war criminal! A killer!

MANUEL
 We're almost there, Carolita!

CAROLITA

A right-wing pig! (*reading from another piece of paper*)
The Six Million Dollar Man! (*throwing the piece of paper*)
You're a capitalist!

MANUEL

Almost there!

CAROLITA

Just listen to your name, you capitalist pig!

MANUEL

And when we get to the other side we'll bathe and find
water to drink and eat real food and wash your shirt and
find you a pill for motion sickness. Okay?

LUPE

(*dancing in the car, to MANUEL*) I'll be Han Solo if
you'll be Princess Leia. No, actually, Luke Skywalker.
(*to CAROLITA*) You can be Darth Vader, you whiny
little bitch.

MANUEL

Hey! I WILL slap!

CAROLITA

(*reading from another piece of paper, to MANUEL*) YOU!
That's right! YOU! Manuel Javier Gonzalez Zurita. YOU!!!

CAROLITA *throws the piece of paper.*

MANUEL

You hate me now, but trust me, once we get to the other
side of the border, you'll thank me forever.

CAROLITA
Will Mom be there?

LUPE
She'll come.

CAROLITA
(*to MANUEL*) If she's not there, I'll HATE you forever.

LUPE
(*pointing ahead, to the wall, which is in 2020*) Dad! There's the wall! It's, like, thirty feet high!

CAROLITA
It's, like, from the future!

LUPE
And it goes on forever!

MANUEL
It DOES look very futuristic. We'll find an opening.

LUPE
You mean a checkpoint?

MANUEL
(*to CAROLITA*) In the deep, anarchist future there will be no walls, because there will be no nation-states and therefore no borders.

LUPE
Is there a checkpoint around?

CAROLITA
No.

MANUEL
(*to LUPE*) Not a checkpoint –

CAROLITA
Let's just turn around and go back.

LUPE
(*to CAROLITA*) To what? –

MANUEL
We don't have our passports.

LUPE
(*to CAROLITA*) Exile?

MANUEL
We only needed my driver's licence to get into the U.S. We
have to find an opening.

LUPE
How will we get through all the other borders without our
passports?

MANUEL
We'll cross that bridge when we come to it. We've been
underground before. In the deep future, girls, there will be
no passports, no exile, no coups.

LUPE
But what are we going to do right now?

MANUEL
We'll figure it out.

LUPE
When is the present over?

CAROLITA
Never!

MANUEL
Everything we need is on the other side of this wall.

CAROLITA
I think it's electrified. I hear a buzzing. And there's a
tingling like a snake up my spine all the way to my tongue.

MANUEL
That's the LIFE! The life on the other side!

LUPE
Are you sure, Dad? It's going to electrocute us if we get
too close.

MANUEL
Oh, my South! The source of so much pain and so much
joy! My SOUTH!

LUPE
I feel a charge running from my fingertips up my arms.

MANUEL
That's the magnetic pull of our beloved South. We just
need to figure out how to get through this fucking wall.

*ABUELO appears above them, in 1979. He is
dressed like the maître d' of a fancy restaurant and
pours water into glasses.*

CAROLITA
You guys! Look! Grandpa's in the sky!

ABUELO
Fly up above it!

CAROLITA
(*waving*) Abuelo!

MANUEL
(*seeing ABUELO*) Don Lautaro?!

CAROLITA
He's saying we should pull a Sandy and Danny and fly
into the sky!

LUPE
Abuelo! I love you so much!

> *CAROLITA sings a line from "We Go Together"*
> *from* Grease *to ABUELO.*

ABUELO
Find some wings and fly!

> *CAROLITA continues singing "We Go Together."*

MANUEL
Don Lautaro, did you die?

ABUELO
Am I a ghost? No! Alive and well in Chile, awaiting
your return!

CAROLITA

Dad, it's the space-time continuum!

ABUELO

Find some wings and fly over it!

LUPE

Maybe we should leave the car behind and just walk, Dad. I don't think there are openings big enough to fit it. Abuelo! Don't go anywhere, just wait for us on the other side, okay?!

ABUELO

Find some wings and fly!

MANUEL

Don Lautaro, however it is that you got here, whatever it is that you're doing, it's incredible to see you, so untouched by the North, entirely of the South!

ABUELO

(*to CAROLITA*) Ask your great-aunt Lili to call on her colony of thousands to pick you up and fly you!

MANUEL

What?

LUPE

(*at the same time as MANUEL*) Who?

CAROLITA

(*singing and looking around*) Great-aunt Lili! Great-aunt Lili! Dad! He's got water!

MANUEL

Yes, Don Lautaro, what are you doing?

ABUELO
   Giving you the strength and hydration to get over this wall.

CAROLITA
   (*choking up*) Grandpa! I haven't seen you in so long! Tata!
   Come down! I want to smell you! Abuelo!

LUPE
   No, Abuelo, just show us the way across, THEN come
   down so we can hug.

CAROLITA
   (*to ABUELO*) I remember you now! (*singing to ABUELO*)
   "We'll always be like one!"

LUPE, CAROLITA and MANUEL
   (*singing to ABUELO*) "Up in the skies above!"

CAROLITA
   Abuelo in the sky! Just pour the water on us!

LUPE
   Yeah!

      They face upwards and open their mouths.
      ABUELO pours the water into their mouths.
      MANUEL looks up to see what's going on.

LUPE
   Dad!!! The wall!!! Dad!!!

      They crash.

Act 2

SCENE 1

The south side of the wall in 2020. We see the backs of OLD MAN WITH EGG, CHICLET SELLER (a tiny four-year-old girl), STRAWBERRY SELLER (a very old lady), FLOOR WAXER (a stooped old man), and FUNERAL-WREATH SELLER (an old man). CHICLET SELLER is held up by STRAWBERRY SELLER, FLOOR WAXER, and GENERAL JUANA AZURDUY DE PADILLA. She looks through a hole in the wall. GENERAL JUANA AZURDUY DE PADILLA is the only one who faces us, wearing the plastic garbage bag. FUNERAL WREATH SELLER faces the wall with his wreaths, as does OLD MAN WITH EGG. El NEGRO MATAPACOS does doggie things throughout the scene. CAROLITA, in 1979, watches from above the wall. She wears monarch-butterfly wings. The others can't see or hear her.

All the vendors sing out their wares in a cacophony before going into the scripted dialogue.

CHICLET SELLER
(*yelling into the hole, her back to us*) Hola!!! Hola!!!

CAROLITA
Hola!

OLD MAN WITH EGG
What do you see?

CHICLET SELLER
A convertible all crashed up with smoke coming out of
it. Right here. A man and a girl are lying on the ground
around it, eyes closed, not moving at all. I don't think
they're breathing. Other than that, nothing.

FLOOR WAXER
No floors for me to wax?

CHICLET SELLER
Nothing at all.

STRAWBERRY SELLER
(*towards the wall, offering her basket of strawberries, in a
singsong voice*) Strawberries! Packed with vitamins, fibre,
and high levels of antioxidants!

CHICLET SELLER
Come out, come out, wherever you are!

CAROLITA
I'm here! Look at me! Wings and all to fly me north with
my great-aunt Lili! She gave these to me!

FLOOR WAXER
(*also towards the wall, in a singsong vendor voice*) Floor
wax: oak wax, linoleum wax, French parquet wax, ceramic
wax, tile wax, birch wax!

GENERAL JUANA AZURDUY DE PADILLA
(*to OLD MAN WITH EGG*) Is that egg for sale?

FLOOR WAXER
(*in a singsong vendor voice*) Floor shined so bright ...

OLD MAN WITH EGG
(to GENERAL JUANA AZURDUY DE PADILLA,
offering the egg) No. You can have it.

FLOOR WAXER
You'll see your own reflection!

STRAWBERRY SELLER
(still in a singsong vendor voice) Strawberries!

CHICLET SELLER
No Life anywhere.

STRAWBERRY SELLER
Sodium-free, fat-free, cholesterol-free, low-calories!

CAROLITA
Hola! (choking up) Why am I a "poor Latina" girl in the
North and an invisible girl in the South? Why? Abuelo?
Great-aunt Lili?

GENERAL JUANA AZURDUY DE PADILLA
(to OLD MAN WITH EGG) But what about you?

OLD MAN WITH EGG
That egg was for my grandson.

STRAWBERRY SELLER
(still in a singsong vendor voice) Strawberries! A good
source of manganese and potassium!

OLD MAN WITH EGG
But he died.

FUNERAL WREATH SELLER
(*to OLD MAN WITH EGG*) My sincerest condolences for
that angel. Would you like to trade the wreath for the egg?

GENERAL JUANA AZURDUY DE PADILLA
(*to WREATH SELLER*) Oh yes, of course, you go ahead.
I'm a ghost, so I shouldn't feel the need to eat, because I'm
not actually here, in this body, although it certainly feels
like I am. Especially now that my stomach is growling. Is
this what's referred to as phantom pain?

OLD MAN WITH EGG gives FUNERAL
WREATH SELLER the egg. FUNERAL WREATH
SELLER gives OLD MAN WITH EGG a wreath.
OLD MAN WITH EGG places the wreath on a
spot and sits with it, praying softly, until the end of
the scene.

FLOOR WAXER
(*in a singsong vendor voice*) Your floor will be like a mirror!

YOUNG MAN WITH A BALLOON IN HIS
HEART, in 2020, climbs the wall from the north.
He holds a red Mickey Mouse–shaped balloon on
a string.

CAROLITA
Hola! Hola!

YOUNG MAN WITH A BALLOON IN HIS
HEART can't see CAROLITA. She pushes him into
the South. He lands perfectly on his feet, thankful
for the push. The rest let CHICLET SELLER down.
Everyone faces the audience now.

YOUNG MAN WITH A BALLOON IN HIS HEART
(*to GENERAL JUANA AZURDUY DE PADILLA and EL
NEGRO MATAPACOS*) Negro Matapacos!

El NEGRO MATAPACOS
(*barking*) "El pueblo unido jamás será vencido."

YOUNG MAN WITH A BALLOON IN HIS HEART
General Juana Azurduy de Padilla!

GENERAL JUANA AZURDUY DE PADILLA
(*shy about her attire, but quickly recovering her dignity*) Is
that an accusation?

YOUNG MAN WITH A BALLOON IN HIS HEART
Oh no! No! I'm a fan. A big, big fan. I just died. Is this
limbo, heaven – I think I just sensed an angel, there was a
fluttering of wings, and the gentle brush of a small hand –
or am I south?

GENERAL JUANA AZURDUY DE PADILLA
We're twenty feet south of the North.

YOUNG MAN WITH A BALLOON IN HIS HEART
Excellent. I got up this morning a healthy twenty-five-year-
old who worked the strawberry fields at the crack of dawn.
Then I clutched my chest in pain. Hours and hours passed
at the hospital. They put a balloon in my damaged heart.
At least my recurring dream will haunt me no more.

GENERAL JUANA AZURDUY DE PADILLA
Oh, I forgot about that. I also had a nightly dream that
stopped haunting me once I passed into this realm. It was
one where I stood naked before myself, my vulva oozing
puss, but the puss was a bed for a garden of calla lilies. All

this puss flowing out of my vagina, and all these flowers sprouting from the stream of puss.

CAROLITA
Sufferin' succotash.

YOUNG MAN WITH A BALLOON IN HIS HEART
In my dream a naked me stands before me, holes where my eyes once were. The holes are dripping blood.

CAROLITA
You two need to watch an episode of *Fantasy Island*.

YOUNG MAN WITH A BALLOON IN HIS HEART
(*to GENERAL JUANA AZURDUY DE PADILLA*) And yes, I would call that phantom pain. Your hunger. The pain of hunger afflicted me many times when I was alive.

STRAWBERRY SELLER
In the NORTH?!

YOUNG MAN WITH A BALLOON IN HIS HEART
The American Dream is nothing but the daily nightmare of work.

STRAWBERRY SELLER
I don't believe you. (*in a singsong vendor voice, towards the other side of the wall*) Plump strawberries!

YOUNG MAN WITH A BALLOON IN HIS HEART
Hunger.

FLOOR WAXER
(*in a singsong vendor voice, towards the other side of the wall*) Your floor will be a glacial lake!

FUNERAL WREATH SELLER
(*to GENERAL JUANA AZURDUY DE PADILLA and
YOUNG MAN WITH A BALLOON IN HIS HEART*)
Would you like wreaths for your graves?

STRAWBERRY SELLER
(*in a singsong voice*) So red!

CHICLET SELLER
(*approaching YOUNG MAN WITH A BALLOON IN HIS
HEART*) Did you get that balloon at Disneyland?

YOUNG MAN WITH A BALLOON IN HIS HEART
No, they put it in my heart at the hospital.

STRAWBERRY SELLER
(*in a singsong vendor voice*) So juicy!

CHICLET SELLER
(*to YOUNG MAN WITH A BALLOON IN HIS HEART*)
Trade it for some gum?

FLOOR WAXER
(*in a singsong vendor voice*) Like walking on water!

YOUNG MAN WITH A BALLOON IN HIS HEART
(*giving balloon to CHICLET SELLER*) Here you go. I'm a
ghost. So I can't chew.

FUNERAL WREATH SELLER
But surely your body is somewhere? Being mourned? And
that body is being buried? By someone? And they want
a wreath?

STRAWBERRY SELLER
(*in a singsong vendor voice*) Fibre!

CHICLET SELLER
(*to STRAWBERRY VENDOR*) Other than the girl and
man lying perfectly still next to the car, with their eyes
closed, not a single sign of Life on the other side.

FUNERAL WREATH SELLER
Then business will be good.

GENERAL JUANA AZURDUY DE PADILLA
The future is here. It always has been.

CAROLITA
It has?

YOUNG MAN WITH A BALLOON IN HIS HEART
Why do you think I'm back?

FUNERAL WREATH SELLER
(*to YOUNG MAN WITH A BALLOON IN HIS HEART*)
Is your body in Phoenix, by any chance? My niece
awaits me there.

YOUNG MAN WITH A BALLOON IN HIS HEART
It's zipped into a black body bag. Somewhere. I don't
remember where. Waiting. For someone. Anyone.

GENERAL JUANA AZURDUY DE PADILLA
Will you walk with me, compañeros? To Antofagasta?
They're erecting a monument in my honour.

YOUNG MAN WITH A BALLOON IN HIS HEART
Of course. What's the strategy?

GENERAL JUANA AZURDUY DE PADILLA
(*to YOUNG MAN WITH A BALLOON IN HIS HEART*)
The strategy is the same one as always: a potent, unified
South. Gringos out. (*referring to all of them*) You are here
(*referring to the North*) because the gringos are there
(*referring to the South*).

El NEGRO MATAPACOS
(*barking*) "El pueblo unido jamás será vencido."

FUNERAL WREATH SELLER
Does your plan include roses with the bread?

GENERAL JUANA AZURDUY DE PADILLA
Always.

FUNERAL WREATH SELLER
(*pulling a rose out of one of the wreaths*) Here's one to get
you started.

FLOOR WAXER
(*in a singsong vendor voice*) Skate on your floors like on a
frozen river!

CHICLET SELLER
(*with EL NEGRO MATAPACOS*) Can we come?

GENERAL JUANA AZURDUY DE PADILLA
Of course.

CAROLITA
(*singing*) "Mujer, semilla fruto, flor, camino! Luchar es
altamente femenino!"

GENERAL JUANA AZURDUY DE PADILLA
takes the hands of CHICLET SELLER and
YOUNG MAN WITH a BALLOON IN HIS
HEART; they walk south with EL NEGRO
MATAPACOS, who barks out "El pueblo unido
jamás será vencido." OLD MAN WITH EGG
continues to pray. FUNERAL WREATH SELLER,
FLOOR WAXER, and STRAWBERRY VENDOR
watch the others leave, then turn towards the wall.

CAROLITA
Why am I invisible in the South?

SCENE 2

The north side of the wall in 1979, although the wall itself is in 2020.

Lights up on LAURA, in 1979, Samsonite and compass in hand.

LAURA

Mother, I know that for you there are only two choices for women: wife slash mother or whore. That's it. But there must be a way, Mother, don't you think, to live in the grey? Not in the black and white.

Beat.

Mother, did you have lovers? Did you dream about leaving my father? Did you wonder what it would have been like to not have to stare down the barrel of a day that could only offer the waxing of floors on all fours, the making of meals from scratch, the scrubbing of your husband's · dirty socks and underwear, the starching of sheets and embroidering of handkerchiefs?

Beat.

Did you ever want to get off the train and walk into the unknown?

LAURA turns her back to the audience and starts to walk.

Give me strength, Aunt Lili, give me strength.

LAURA sings lines from Claudio Ittura and Sergio Ortega's "Venceremos."

CAROLITA still sits on the wall, facing south, her back to us. She turns around, straddling the wall.

CAROLITA
(*looking south*) If I claim you, South, will you claim me too? If I leave the North, when will I arrive at you? Does the leaving ever end? Does the arrival ever begin?

A posse of monarch butterflies appears over the wall, from the South, in 2020. They help FUNERAL WREATH SELLER and FLOOR WAXER over the wall.

FUNERAL WREATH SELLER and FLOOR WAXER walk north. They pass LAURA. She sees them.

MANUEL and LUPE are lying unconscious around the car. Smoke wafts from the convertible's engine.

MANUEL
(*coming to*) What happened?

CAROLITA
(*turning completely to the North*) We crashed.

MANUEL
We're dead?

LUPE
(*coming to, seeing CAROLITA with wings on*) How come YOU get the wings in the afterlife?

CAROLITA
We're alive, duh.

LUPE
Oh.

MANUEL
My girls are okay?

LUPE and CAROLITA
Yes, Dad.

LUPE
(*noticing the car*) Our car's a third-generation Eldorado
Cadillac convertible! How the –

MANUEL
How did you get up to the top of the wall?

CAROLITA
(*referring to the wings*) Great-Aunt Lili gave these to me.
Her and Abuelo made it happen.

MANUEL
(*looking around*) Don Lautaro?! Don Lautaro!

CAROLITA
He's gone now.

MANUEL
(*noticing the car for the first time*) Why is our car a hot-
pink convertible?

CAROLITA
It transformed days ago.

MANUEL
What?

LUPE
Dad, the car – wherever it came from – is broken now.

MANUEL
(*to CAROLITA*) Come down, we need to find an opening.

CAROLITA
Dad! The South is beautiful and ours, and people sing
when they talk and they make friends on the spot and the
poor people share everything and you talk about the crux
right away, like, even with total strangers at the market,
just like you always said. And I can imagine it now the way
you and the other adults describe it, like how people let
their thighs rub next to yours on the buses, and how you
dance cumbia whenever the urge hits you, and how people
make out on plaza benches and traffic islands and even
while they're protesting they're making out. But nobody
can see us there. (*turning to face the South again, waving
arms*) Hola! Hola! Hola! (*turning back*) See? Full of Life,
just like you've always said, but I'm invisible to them.

> *MANUEL starts to weep.*

CAROLITA
(*climbing down into the North*) Dad, don't cry.

> *MANUEL walks away from the car, weeping,
> trying to assess the situation. LUPE and
> CAROLITA follow. LUPE carries her unicorn stuffy.
> CAROLITA still wears her laundromat heels.*

LUPE
(*rubbing MANUEL's back*) Dad, everything's gonna be okay. We'll find help somewhere.

Lights up on a shrine made of shoes, animal skulls, baseball caps, and found objects of migrants. It's the size of their car. The shrine is in 2020. LUPE, CAROLITA, and MANUEL take it in.

LUPE
What is that?

MANUEL
A shrine. Made of the found objects of migrants.

LUPE
Wow.

CAROLITA
So the people who made it are, like, religious fanatics?

MANUEL
No, they use some Catholic symbols, but their spiritual beliefs date back thousands of years, before the Church came to these shores, before this was the States, before this was Mexico, before this was a border. Did you girls know that a hundred years ago, this actually WAS Mexico? Before the gringos stole this land?

LUPE
So, like, why did people make this shrine?

MANUEL
To remember a migrant that died here. And then other migrants passing through have added to it. To honour this

person's journey, which represents the journey of so many others. To say, "I see you."

> *LUPE adds her unicorn to the shrine. CAROLITA adds her wings, then her shoes.*

LUPE
Dad, add that envelope of Chilean soil that Grandma sent you. The one you always carry in your shirt pocket, right next to your heart.

MANUEL
I can't.

SCENE 3

MAN WITH TV DINNER shows up. He is in 1973.

MAN WITH TV DINNER
Excuse me.

CAROLITA
Who are you, and why are you wearing a suit and a
hairstyle from, like, six years ago?

MAN WITH TV DINNER
I seem to be lost. (*referring to the shrine*) That's the most
stunning shrine I've ever seen. There's so many since the
coup, but that one is the most breathtaking.

MAN WITH TV DINNER crosses himself.

MAN WITH TV DINNER
(*to all of them*) I'm sorry for your loss.

MANUEL
Who are you?

MAN WITH TV DINNER
I'm looking for a Bill O'Neill.

MANUEL
The fucking hippie?!

MAN WITH TV DINNER
He's at the stadium.

LUPE
Hey! Did you see our mom?

MAN WITH TV DINNER
At the Canadian embassy?

MANUEL
Okay, girls. The electric charge coming off this wall – is it
just me or is it louder now? – is giving us shock therapy.

MAN WITH TV DINNER
There were a lot of people jumping the embassy wall.
What was her name?

CAROLITA and LUPE
Laura Carolina Torres Perez.

LUPE
How do you just jump the wall?

MAN WITH TV DINNER
Well, it's not that difficult, really, I suppose, if you manage
to get past the tanks – sorry, but where's the stadium? I
need to get there before the gravy curdles.

LUPE
That smells so good. What is it?

MAN WITH TV DINNER
Steak, potatoes, peas, and corn. That's the gravy there. And
this is an orange juice.

MANUEL
So we're ALL seeing this vision, right? You girls are seeing
this guy, and we can ALL smell this food and hear him talk

about the fucking hippie? (*mostly to himself*) Maybe we all have brain damage from the crash.

MAN WITH TV DINNER
The embassy car left me back there, what with all the roadblocks –

MANUEL
How do you know Bill O'Neill, Mr. Vision?

MAN WITH TV DINNER
I don't. He registered at the embassy when he arrived, and now he's managed to get himself arrested –

CAROLITA
Bill O'Neill is in JAIL? For making out with Mom?

LUPE
Grab a brain. Making out is not a CRIME –

MAN WITH TV DINNER
I think it had more to do with the long hair and the beard. Also, he was at the New Havana shantytown helping build houses.

MANUEL
(*paranoid, to the girls*) Okay, how does this guy know all of this? Where do you think you are, Mr. Vision?

MAN WITH TV DINNER
Santiago.

MANUEL
Santiago!

LUPE
Oh! Dad! He's a hologram from another place, another
era, another time zone, another hemisphere, another life,
another reality –

CAROLITA
We get it, already.

LUPE
(*giving CAROLITA the finger, talking to MANUEL*)
Another experience, another geography, another –

MANUEL
Get to your point, Lupe.

CAROLITA
(*giving LUPE the finger*) Show-off, show-off, nothin' but
a show-off!

    LUPE gives CAROLITA the finger.

LUPE
Dad, do you think we fell into a space-time continuum
black hole when we crashed?

CAROLITA
No, this wall's fantastical –

LUPE
"Fantastical"? Excuse me while I go puke.

CAROLITA
(*giving LUPE the finger*) There was a guy on the other side
with a Mickey Mouse balloon for a heart –

MANUEL
We may all have concussions.

LUPE
(*to MAN WITH TV DINNER*) What's the date?

MAN WITH TV DINNER
September 30, 1973.

MANUEL
And you're in Santiago?

MAN WITH TV DINNER
I see it now. The stadium. Surrounded by tanks, jeeps, military men. (*referring to the sound of a helicopter*) There are helicopters.

LUPE
(*looking up at the helicopter, which is actually in 2020*) No, that's right here, right now.

MAN WITH TV DINNER
There are hundreds of desperate women with children, elderly people, lined up, clamouring for their men.

MANUEL
What else do you see?

MAN WITH TV DINNER
A green military bus pulling up. With prisoners. Fresh from the shantytowns, with students, and some men in suits, yes, some middle-class people too.

LUPE
What's happening to them?

MAN WITH TV DINNER
> They're blindfolded, hands behind their heads, being
> pushed and prodded into the stadium, with the soldiers'
> rifle butts. Many of the men aren't men. They are boys.
> Teenaged boys. The families waiting outside cry.

LUPE
> Are there women?

MAN WITH TV DINNER
> Yes. Señoras wearing their aprons, their hands still covered
> with flour. Blindfolded, hands behind their heads. Women
> with babies in their arms, blindfolded. Women holding
> their blindfolded children's hands.

MANUEL
> (*covering his ears*) No. No.

LUPE
> It's okay, Dad. These things happen.

MAN WITH TV DINNER
> Tabarnak!

CAROLITA
> The helicopter's right above us now. (*waving*) Hey! Can
> you help us? We crashed! (*to the others*) It's supersonic,
> like, from way in the future!

MANUEL
> You're looking for Bill in the stadium?

MAN WITH TV DINNER
> Yes.

MANUEL
　You're bringing him that TV dinner?

MAN WITH TV DINNER
　Yes, he's been held there for fifteen days now. I finally
　tracked him down.

MANUEL
　I know who you are! Bill never talks about his time
　in the stadium, but he mentioned your name! Michel
　Trépannier!

MAN WITH TV DINNER
　Yes!

CAROLITA
　(*still waving at the helicopter, but introjecting*) How
　old is Bill?

MAN WITH TV DINNER
　Twenty-one. Bill O'Neill, from Burnaby, BC, son of
　a longshoreman. Here in Santiago for a year now.
　Member of the Chilean Movement of the Revolutionary
　Left. The MIR.

MANUEL
　The MIR? A true internationalist.

LUPE
　Why aren't you bringing the other prisoners TV dinners?

MAN WITH TV DINNER
　Because they're not Canadians.

CAROLITA
(*still waving at the helicopter with one hand, giving MAN WITH TV DINNER the finger with the other*)
Fuck you, you selfish, racist, individualist, nationalistic, right-wing pig.

MAN WITH TV DINNER
Uh, I'm smuggling this dinner into the stadium behind the ambassador's back. He got word from Pierre Elliott Trudeau that Canada is FOR Pinochet's coup. I'm doing this of my own volition. When I get caught – and it's not a question of IF, but a question of WHEN – I'll be fired and never work in diplomacy again. So, as much as I'd love to bring food to all the prisoners –

ARCANGEL
(*offstage, in a loud whisper*) Help!

MANUEL
Did you hear that?

ARCANGEL
(*offstage*) Help!

CAROLITA
(*still waving at the helicopter*) Come out, come out, wherever you are!

MAN WITH TV DINNER
Is it Bill O'Neill? Perhaps he's waiting at the gate?

The helicopter continues on its way.

CAROLITA
(*to the helicopter*) No, no! Helicopter! Come back
and help us!

ARCANGEL *appears.*

ARCANGEL
(*to CAROLITA*) Shhh! That helicopter is looking for me.

CAROLITA
Right now, in 1979?

ARCANGEL
No, right now, in 2020.

CAROLITA
(*referring to the helicopter*) I knew it was from the
deep future!

MANUEL
(*mostly to himself*) None of my peers will ever believe any
of this. (*to ARCANGEL*) Fuck! You're dehydrated! (*to
MAN WITH TV DINNER*) Give him the orange juice –

MAN WITH TV DINNER
I'd love to, but if you had any idea of everything I've had
to do to come this far for Bill O'Neill –

CAROLITA
Imperialist!

CAROLITA *grabs the orange juice and gives it
to ARCANGEL. He downs it in one big, huge
gulp, puts the empty container on the shrine, and
crosses himself.*

CAROLITA
(*to ARCANGEL*) Hey, in 2020, is the Bionic Woman
married to a PIG – Pretty Intelligent Girl – who's a Braniff
stewardess?

ARCANGEL
I don't know who that is –

LUPE
And there's obviously still nation-states and borders
and walls?

ARCANGEL
Worse than ever.

LUPE
Oh.

MAN WITH TV DINNER
(*to ARCANGEL*) If you want asylum, you have to go to
the embassy and try to scale the wall –

MANUEL
Where are you coming from?

ARCANGEL
Honduras.

MAN WITH TV DINNER
Oh, THAT embassy is packed.

MANUEL
(*to ARCANGEL*) Still unliberated?

ARCANGEL

We've tried, and we'll keep trying, but the gringos keep
intervening.

MANUEL

What about Chile?

ARCANGEL

Eco-socialist. The president is a Mapuche woman by the
name of Fresia Mali Pillan.

MANUEL

(*weeping with joy, to the sky*) Yes! Yes! Yes! Until the Final
Victory Always!

MAN WITH TV DINNER, LUPE, and CAROLITA

Always.

MANUEL

Yes! The Great Avenues opened once again!

MAN WITH TV DINNER, LUPE, and CAROLITA

Once again.

MANUEL

Lucho, it wasn't for nothing! It wasn't for nothing! Yes! We
have to go back right away.

LUPE

Yes.

> *He continues to weep with joy and longing.*
> *CAROLITA and LUPE hug him.*

MAN WITH TV DINNER
(*to ARCANGEL*) Now, please don't try scaling our wall during curfew. A few people have been shot trying to do that, and it's been covered in blood and bits of brains.

LUPE
(*to ARCANGEL*) What's your name?

ARCANGEL
(*secretively, checking to make sure the helicopter isn't circling back*) Never mind.

MANUEL
The helicopter's gone. Would you like to sit in our car, have a rest?

ARCANGEL studies MANUEL carefully.

LUPE
(*to ARCANGEL*) He's not with the migra.

CAROLITA
And he's not a murderer, although he IS a socialist revolutionary. So that means he believes in armed struggle but only in defensive situations and only against the military.

MANUEL
Shhh! Remember the Canadian government took us in only after we signed a paper agreeing to renounce our leftist activities. We don't know who these people really are –

LUPE
(*referring to MAN WITH TV DINNER*) Well, that one's a
disoriented rebel diplomat from six years ago, (*referring to
ARCANGEL*) and this one's a migrant from four decades
from now.

CAROLITA
Let's just say it: My dad is also in the Movement of
the Revolutionary Left. (*fist in air, chanting*) Pueblo,
conciencia, fusil, MIR, MIR!

MANUEL covers CAROLITA's mouth.

CAROLITA
(*with MANUEL's hand over her mouth*) Pueblo,
conciencia, fusil, MIR, MIR!

MAN WITH TV DINNER
(*to MANUEL*) Did you manage to escape the
firing squad?

MANUEL
Yes! No! I mean, yes, obviously, but I didn't manage to
escape exile. So here you fucking find me, in exile land, for
fuck's sake. (*to the sky*) Why? Why?!

LUPE
Dad! Stop asking God stuff! We don't believe in him!

MANUEL
This border is tampering with all of my beliefs.

LUPE
(*to ARCANGEL, referring to MAN WITH TV DINNER*)
That gringo's from 1973. He's not after you.

ARCANGEL
Okay. I might sit down.

MAN WITH TV DINNER
Which part of the stadium are you coming from, the field
or the tunnels of its underbelly?

He gives ARCANGEL the dinner. As ARCANGEL
devours it:

MAN WITH TV DINNER
Maybe you saw Bill O'Neill? They're giving me the
runaround here at the entrance. Was he with you on the
bleachers, or possibly in the change rooms? Maybe you
saw him in a lineup? He's a Canadian with long hair and a
beard, although they might have shaved his head –

MANUEL
Comrade, how long have you been walking?

ARCANGEL
Thirty-five days. Mostly with the beast. But I crossed the
border four days ago. There were twelve of us. No food,
no water. Some lay down to die yesterday. I continued. My
toenails have fallen off.

MAN WITH TV DINNER
Yes, yes. I've heard the torture is terrible.

MANUEL
He walked here from Honduras, a country ravaged by the
likes of Columbus and Cortés, the United Fruit Company,
and U.S. troops, with their army base there. A country that
has long fought to free itself of those shackles, and in the

anarchist future it will finally triumph because history is
never over –

*ARCANGEL raps, accompanied by an original
musical composition.*

ARCANGEL
    You never know when the beast is gonna go
    Whistle blows, steam shows
    Then it takes off slow

    Within minutes the thing begins:
    Covered in limbs
    Men and women with their
    Wind-whipped skin
    Some kin
    Some unborn
    Some old as abuelos, abuelas
    From slums no different than favelas

    Need and despair is the fuel
    The beast feeds on
    It eats arms and legs
    And crushes heads
    To keep strong

    The train of the dead
    Leaving hundreds slain
    Still those that gain a spot
    Take pains to remain

    You don't wanna get left behind
    Someone's always next in line
    Hundred and fifty crammed on top of a car
    It's death defying. It is death defying.

At times, we have to wait ten hours before
The beast goes
Lethal: beware the eagle's eyes
Through the peepholes

We're people!
But guess some cargo's more precious
The ones with armed guards in every car
Don't let us
Muy cara
La entrada

Once I sat next to a mara
Shitting my pants
Every single inch we advanced
You know porque ...
The maras –
Created in El Norte
Exported by the gringos
Will kill their kinfolk
See, I left Honduras
When the maras –
Said they'd kill me
If I didn't join:
The innocent treated like we're guilty
Plus the politics are filthy

Since the U.S. coup
In '09
When we tried to retake
Our resources
They resorted
To recourses like
Shutting down schools

When students stood up
Armed forces were remorseless
Turned tens of thousands to corpses – Oh God!
No jobs left
So I had to go
On this "magic" road
On this path going
Fast and slow
Battered soul –

I was filthy
Wind whipped my face with no mercy
Cold chilled my bones
And every part of me was thirsty
Every part of me hurt
The very heart of me was bursting!

I took nine trains
Because the beast is not one
It's like a snake made of many
His body is never done
See, living here
Is to live in fear
Of falling from the roof
Getting ground up by the wheels
It's fear of all of the abuse
There are gangs and squads
That rape women and rob
El tren de la muerte, hope for buena suerte
Hundred miles an hour, the cars move side to side
Those asleep when the beast stops suddenly, would collide
So many try and so few survive
Where the train tracks cross
Some were crucified

No pennies or pesos
For beans and huevos
So much help, though
Like from
Señoras in los pueblos
Las Patronas
They would run beside the train
In their aprons
And when the beast slowed down
They raced in
With a bit of water bottled in old plastic
Tamales wrapped in old newspaper package
Warm eyes and their smiles with missing teeth
Were brief relief from the misery
Bittersweet, alongside them
Children running and waving
Soon after that it was time for us to wade in

El Rio Bravo was swollen when I arrived at its shores
Never tried this before, but I had to go in
Learned to float as a boy, but never learned how to swim
So I waited five days at its edge till it shrunk
Hidden in a bush
As patrols passed in speed boats
Searching for illegals
They mockingly call "amigos"

Put my pack on my head
Took a deep breath and stepped
In the depths
The currents pushed me far to the left
This river's deceptive
Surface calm, but below
The currents nearly submerging
Powerful undertow

Nearly died
But somehow reached the other side
This side
Almost couldn't believe I survived
Arrived in El Norte
But not for the dream
Just looking for a job
In this new regime

Where border police lie in wait
Last count was twenty thousand
Chasing all of the escaped
All us wetbacks
On bikes and boats
With cars and jetpacks
In planes, helicopters, and blimps
Laying the death trap
In trucks and jeeps
In the bush and in the streets
So we push
And we shush
And we look
As we creep ...

I scuttled through a tunnel
And at the end was a huddle
A coyote and his group
Patrols still in pursuit
Handed over a roll
Like a different kind of toll
Then looked over the road
For anyone that might hassle

In the daytime I had to move fast
Shadow to shadow

Every single step was a battle
Even under cover of dark
They still search through
Last night, I saw a plane
Silently circle
Lower and lower
With just a light blinking purple
There's so many ways they can hurt you

I was sure I was caught
About to get locked in a box
Key tossed and lost
The police always stalk
And on the beast I was told the cells
Were cold as hell ...
Something they called the Freezer
Where you get covered in tin foil
Instead of blankets
Every single second I felt anxious

CAROLITA
(to ARCANGEL) Be my uncle. Come with us, towards the
magnetic North. We'll bring our pieces of the South there.
Maybe my Abuelo will join us and my Abuela too. Help
me talk my dad into going to Vancouver, the land of cherry
blossoms, where my mom is. He wants to go back to Chile.

MANUEL
More than ever now!

LUPE
Me too.

ARCANGEL

(*to MANUEL*) Oh. (*to CAROLITA*) Thank you. I am
the very centre of a double magnet. One pulls me north,
but the other pulls me south, back to Honduras, a place I
never thought I'd miss. But I do now. With every corner of
my soul. The monarch butterfly whispered my name in my
ear: Arcangel, Arcangel, Arcangel, to remind me who I am
and where I come from.

> *MANUEL and ARCANGEL look at each other
> and start weeping.*

> *ARCANGEL starts to sing Armando Manzanero's
> "Esta tarde vi llover." Gradually MANUEL,
> CAROLITA, and LUPE join in. MAN WITH TV
> DINNER intersperses English translations, singing
> à la Tony Bennett or Barry White. (This is heartfelt
> and real. Absolutely no irony.)*

> *LUPE and CAROLITA take a moment to
> acknowledge each other.*

> *CAROLITA'S DOPPELGÄNGER enters, wearing
> pink wings and riding a festooned banana-seat
> bike. Cherry blossoms fall on her. She sings lines
> from Cheryl Lynn's disco song "Got to Be Real."
> CAROLITA joins in. The two sing a few lines
> together.*

> *ARCANGEL follows CAROLITA'S
> DOPPELGÄNGER offstage.*

> *At the same time, LUPE'S DOPPELGÄNGER
> dances a Brazilian batucada while wearing a kilt
> and holding a bouquet of pink roses. A batucada*

*song takes over the space as MAN WITH TV
DINNER places the empty TV dinner tray on the
shrine and crosses himself. He takes off his shoes and
places them next to the shrine for a migrant who
might need them. He looks up at the wall, climbs it,
and jumps to the other side, landing in the South.*

*MANUEL, LUPE, and CAROLITA get back into
the car and start driving along the wall, looking for
an opening.*

*LAURA comes upon the shrine. She finds the purple
unicorn stuffy and the heels. She looks around. She
opens her Samsonite, takes out her notebook of
poetry, and places it on the shrine. She keeps going.*

SCENE 4

Moments later. MANUEL, LUPE, and CAROLITA
are driving along the wall in 1979. The wall is
from 2020.

LAURA appears, running, carrying her baby-blue
Samsonite and her compass.

LAURA
STOP!!! STOP!!!

CAROLITA
Oh, my God, you guys! It's Mom! She's here!

LUPITA
It's Mom! It's Mom! (*to CAROLITA*) Toldja she was
on her way!

CAROLITA
(*doing an elaborate high-five with LUPE*) YAY!!! The
maternal instinct exists!

MANUEL
Laura?!

LAURA jumps into the back seat of the car and
takes CAROLITA and LUPE in her arms.

LAURA
Oh, my precious, precious babies. (*to all of them*) Where
did this car come from?!

CAROLITA and LUPE
We don't know.

CAROLITA
It's magic.

LAURA
Oh. (*to MANUEL*) You asshole! You're lucky I don't sue you for kidnapping.

CAROLITA
That's what I said!

MANUEL
(*stopping the car, to LAURA*) Get out of the car.

CAROLITA
Dad! She ran all the way here. And if she gets out of the car, I'll get out too. I'll go on strike from being your kidnapped daughter. What about you, Lupe?

LUPE
You can only go on strike if you're a worker against the means of production.

CAROLITA
No, REproduction!

MANUEL
What?!

LUPE
Dad, she ran all the way here.

Beat.

MANUEL

(*getting out of the car, to LAURA*) No one will ever love you like I have loved you. You know that, don't you?

LAURA

Manuel, let's not do this in front of the girls.

MANUEL

I gave everything up for you. I can't believe I got kicked out of my soon-to-be-liberated country for you. (*to the gods*) What the fuck was I thinking?

LUPE

You did it to keep the family together –

CAROLITA

(*to MANUEL*) What do you mean? –

MANUEL

I mean that your mother was the one they wanted. Dead or alive. Not me. Not us. We could have stayed.

CAROLITA

But Dad, the magnet pulled us north, the force of it was for a reason, we can catch up to Arcangel and take him with us to Vancouver –

LUPE

You're making no sense, you stupid fool.

LAURA

(*to CAROLITA and LUPE*) I didn't die. I lived. For you, all for you. And we decided to go into exile until we can go back.

LUPE
Dad, you did it to keep us all together.

LAURA
(*to MANUEL*) And you found solace in Tita's arms at the refugee hotel. So stop playing the martyr.

LUPE
What?

MANUEL
Hey! Not in front of the girls.

LUPE
Yes, in front of us. Yes!

CAROLITA
It's our right to know the truth!

LUPE
(*getting out of the car*) Before you left for Maria's commune, Mom, you would hide out in my bed at night, and you, Dad, would come and get her, and I heard everything. I was awake. I heard the pleading, the begging, the suicide threats –

CAROLITA
Dad! You were gonna kill yourself over Mom?

LUPE
Yes.

LAURA
Your Dad was in pain.

LUPE

And leave us all behind. (*to MANUEL*) It's not fair to kidnap us over Bill if you had an affair when you were still with Mom, Dad!

MANUEL

I didn't have an affair, and it wasn't a kidnapping –

CAROLITA

(*writing in her notebook*) I'm writing down all the names of all the people who were never fit to be parents. (*ripping a page out of her notebook*) Darth Vader. (*ripping a page out of her notebook*) Joan Crawford

MANUEL

In the not-so-deep future –

CAROLITA

Stop TALKING about the future and go get it for us, already!

MANUEL

You'll like what I'm about to say: We scientists – maybe even you, Lupe! – will invent a communications tool where you will be able to share your thoughts with the whole world by typing them onto a computer screen and pressing a button. It's already in the works, actually, at MIT –

CAROLITA

(*ripping a page out of her notebook*) Manuel Javier Gonzalez Zurita.

MANUEL

Engineers may even invent flying cars by then.

CAROLITA

(*ripping a page out of her notebook*) Laura Carolina
Torres Perez.

MANUEL

To get us over these walls.

CAROLITA

Dad! We were going to be bastards!

LUPE

Bastard is when a woman has kids out of wedlock.

LAURA

Your father was just saying that.

LUPE

(*to CAROLITA*) He wasn't going to kill himself.

LAURA

(*to MANUEL*) Manuel, this is not the time for your
science musings.

LUPE

(*to CAROLITA*) People will say anything to make their
lovers feel sorry for them, duh.

CAROLITA

You think you're so great.

LAURA

Funny how that sexist pig Sigmund Freud called women
hysterical, but look at what your father did: threatened
suicide, took you girls away from their mother. Now he's

saying he would rather have stayed in Chile all by himself instead of raising his girls. See? See?

MANUEL gets into the car. LAURA gets out, gets LUPE, and puts her in the back. LAURA gets in the front passenger seat. MANUEL starts the car and begins driving along the wall again.

LAURA
What are you doing?

MANUEL
Driving. South. With everyone. (*to CAROLITA*) To go get the eco-socialist future, Carolita! (*to LAURA*) We're going back to join the struggle. We know the triumph is coming.

LAURA
We can't.

MANUEL
Yes. We can go underground.

LAURA
We'll be killed. Or worse.

CAROLITA
What's worse than dying?

LUPE
Torture. Like, duh.

CAROLITA
Or maybe exile?

LAURA

(*privately, to MANUEL only*) We've had this discussion before. We will not put our girls in danger.

MANUEL

(*to LAURA*) You already did that when you took up arms at the university and held down the fort with your students.

LAURA

(*to MANUEL*) Excuse me?!

CAROLITA

(*to LUPE*) I met a murderer on this trip.

LUPE

(*to CAROLITA*) Liar.

CAROLITA

(*to LUPE*) When we'd stopped to sleep.

LUPE

So why are you still alive then, Einstein?

CAROLITA

'Cuz he liked me. And he only kills desperate brown people coming north, not going south.

MANUEL

(*to LAURA*) And by the way, I know you fucked Julio, that Che Guevara–wannabe with the beret –

LAURA

(*to MANUEL*) What the?! –

MANUEL

(*to LAURA*) You weren't tutoring him. You almost got yourself killed on the day of the coup to impress that little rich boy playing proletariat, what with the perpetual strumming of the guitar and Victor Jara songs. At least Bill's working class and a true comrade.

CAROLITA

(*to LUPE*) I had to raise my hands in the air while he pointed one of his guns at me.

LUPE

(*to CAROLITA*) Right. And Tony Orlando and Dawn came to me at the drive-thru and sang "He Don't Love You (Like I Love You)."

LAURA

(*to MANUEL*) What the hell are you talking about?

MANUEL

(*to LAURA*) Don't play dumb with me.

LAURA

(*to MANUEL*) Have you lost your fucking mind?

MANUEL

(*to LAURA*) I know your tricks.

CAROLITA

(*to LUPE*) And I put a spell on him to put down his guns.

MANUEL

(*to LAURA still*) You pathologize me when I speak a truth.

CAROLITA

(*to LUPE*) And he did.

LUPE

(*to CAROLITA*) Right. Did you cross your arms and nod like Jeannie or twitch your nose like Samantha?

CAROLITA

(*to LUPE*) Fuck you!

LAURA

(*to MANUEL*) You know very well that I took up arms on the day of the coup and did everything I did for our girls' future.

> *LUPE and CAROLITA give each other the finger and say "fuck you" to each other over and over again throughout the next beat of dialogue.*

MANUEL

(*to LAURA*) Do you see what I've had to put up with for days while you make out with Bill?

LAURA

(*to MANUEL*) Welcome to what millions of women put up with day in and day out.

MANUEL

(*to LUPE and CAROLITA*) Stop, or there will be no *Bionic Woman* or *Star Trek*!

> *LUPE and CAROLITA stop.*

LAURA

(*to MANUEL*) Did you hear what I said earlier? I know all about Tita.

MANUEL

(*to LAURA*) You're paranoid, you know that?

LAURA

You think I'm an idiot? I smelled it on you, I read it on your face, in both of your eyes.

LUPE

You mean like ACTUAL Aunt Tita? Like TITA Tita?

CAROLITA

Dad! That's so gross.

LUPE

I know. She's like our family. Well, so is Bill for that matter.

CAROLITA

No, it's gross 'cuz she has, like, a moustache and she's, like, a bitch.

LAURA

Don't call women "bitches."

CAROLITA

But what if they are?

MANUEL

She does not have a moustache.

CAROLITA

Does too.

MANUEL
Nothing happened with Aunt Tita. We talked a lot. That's
all. You know, about the situation with her husband.

LUPE
So it was an EMOTIONAL affair?

CAROLITA
Huh?

LAURA
(*to MANUEL*) How does she know that concept?

LUPE
Her husband was drunk all the time because of the
concentration camps. He needed to drown his sorrows.

MANUEL
(*to LAURA*) How does she know that? Did you
tell her that?

LAURA
Of course not.

CAROLITA
Hello! We have EARS, crazy people!

LUPE
They're not crazy –

CAROLITA
We can hear all you guys talking about all your affairs and
stuff and the tortures!

LUPE

They're just in exile.

CAROLITA

Like, they kept stuffing Uncle Leonel's naked body into little boxes so he developed a phobia of being enclosed and that's why he would drink bottles of rum and run around Stanley Park until the cops caught him and put him in the jail at Powell and Gore and they hit him 'cuz they thought he was "just another drunk Indian." Those are the words the police used on him: "drunk Indian," 'cuz the cops are racists and instruments of the powers at be.

LAURA

(to MANUEL) You and Tita were not just talking. And given everything that we've all been through, I didn't blame you.

MANUEL

How's Bill the homewrecker?

CAROLITA

Did he wreck the house?!

LUPE

Fuck, you're so dumb. Homewrecker is like when the husband or wife has an affair with somebody, and the lover wrecks the home.

CAROLITA

Like, burns it down?

LUPE

It's a metaphor! He didn't ACTUALLY wreck the house!

MANUEL

Bill is a homewrecker because he destroyed our family by
taking your mother away from us.

LAURA

Because I'm an object, girls. I just let men take me
from one place to the other. I don't have any of my own
thoughts or feelings. I don't make any of my own choices. I
have no agency whatsoever in any given situation.

LUPE

The point is that both of you slept with other people.

MANUEL

(*to LAURA*) You're in love with him, right?

CAROLITA

Or is he in love with you, Mom?

LUPE

Shut up.

LAURA

Define "love."

CAROLITA

It's like when two people want to lick each other like
lollipops all the time and –

LUPE

Ewwww! Not YOU. DAD.

MANUEL.

Just answer the fucking question: Are you in
love with him?

LAURA

I'm not trying to be difficult. I'm asking a real question:
Define "love." Is it giving everything up for someone?
Even your own identity? Is it renouncing your beliefs? Is it
losing yourself so entirely in someone else that you forget
who you are?

MANUEL

Or following someone into exile?

Beat.

What you're saying is that you don't love me anymore.

LAURA

(*to MANUEL*) What I'm saying is that I met you when I
was sixteen.

CAROLITA

Were you a virgin when you met him, Mom?

LAURA

Uh –

MANUEL

Oh, just fucking tell them your whole life story now, like
they're your girlfriends and not your daughters. Just be
their friend, not their mother. Hell, I'll do it for you! Girls,
your mother had had lots of boyfriends already and she'd
been sleeping with the last one. So no, she wasn't a virgin.
She was a veteran heartbreaker, in fact. You just broke Bill's
heart too, didn't you?

LAURA
I was sixteen. A child. I thought I knew everything. I'm not a child anymore.

MANUEL
And you're in love with Bill.

LAURA
I don't know.

LUPE
Mom! Do you know if you're still in love with Dad?

LAURA
I will always love your father.

CAROLITA
Just not like a lollipop?

LAURA
That's hard to sustain.

LUPE
What?

MANUEL
She's saying it's hard to want to suck the same lollipop for your whole life.

CAROLITA
I can think of one bionic lollipop I want to suck forever and ever and ever.

LUPE
Excuse me while I go puke.

CAROLITA
(*to LUPE*) Stop pretending to be such a fucking priss. Tavito told me all about spin the bottle and how you sucked on Rodrigo's tongue like it was a Fudgesicle.

MANUEL
Rodrigo?

CAROLITA
Yes!

MANUEL
Gutierrez?

LUPE
Yes!

MANUEL
(*to LAURA*) Did you know about this?

LAURA
No. (*to LUPE and CAROLITA*) Lupe, you'll get your period soon. Whatever you decide to do is fine, as long as you don't get pregnant. So you'll tell me when you start sleeping with boys, and we'll go to the doctor and get you the pill.

MANUEL
I can't believe this.

LUPE
She's talking about my means of reproduction, Dad.

LAURA
You want her to get pregnant?

MANUEL
Of course not, it's just –

LAURA
What?

MANUEL
Look at her, Laura. LOOK at her. She's a little girl!

LAURA
Who will get her period soon.

MANUEL
That doesn't mean she'll start having sex, for fuck's sake!

LAURA
But what if she does?

MANUEL
Lupe, please wait till you're at least sixteen, okay?

LAURA
But what if she doesn't?

MANUEL
She will.

LAURA
And if she doesn't? You really want HER to go through
an abortion?

Beat.

MANUEL
Let's just talk about something else.

LAURA

No. (*to LUPE*) You will tell us when you start having sex,
no matter how young you are, and we will get you the pill.

LUPE

Okay, Mom.

Beat.

LUPE

(*mostly to herself*) My childhood is over, isn't it?

CAROLITA

(*mostly to herself*) The future will never come, will it?

LAURA

(*to LUPE AND CAROLITA*) There is a sacred part of
you that will always remain a child. And you, you are
the future.

MANUEL stops driving.

MANUEL

(*mostly to himself*) I'm all alone, aren't I?

LAURA

(*to MANUEL*) You're softer. I can see that. It's the kind of
softness that can only come through the unseen, unpaid,
isolating, embarrassing, totally exhausting work that is
parenting.

Beat.

(*mostly to herself*) And I'm naked. Spent from what that
chase did to me.

LAURA, MANUEL, LUPE, and CAROLITA hold hands and cry.

CAROLITA

(*pointing*) What's that?

LUPE

What?

MANUEL

It's a superior mirage.

LAURA

You can see it too?

THE VIRGIN CARMEN appears.

THE VIRGIN CARMEN

I am the Virgen Carmen, Goddess of Peruvian Creoles, patron saint of the Plurinational State of Bolivia and of Colombian taxi drivers. I intercept the souls of purgatory who dare to attempt to return to the material realm, I guard the borders and guide the armies of Spain, Chile, Argentina, and Venezuela. I know you don't believe in me, being Marxist-Leninist atheists and all. I know you are offended at the belief in Madonnas, Virgins, or Goddesses, being radical feminists. So chock this apparition up to your imaginations, your delusions, your dreams and nightmares, your fatigue, explain it how you will with your dialectical materialism or physics conclusions that reduce me to a mere optical phenomenon. In short, make sense of my miraculous apparition in your life at the U.S.–Mexico border however you want, but the truth is that I am here with all my armies and the borders that they guard, and I am not a socialist revolutionary. I am of the right. That's right. I am ultra-right-wing. I am loyal to the army, I ask no questions, officialist Virgin that I am. Seven years from now, in 1986, when a bazooka is aimed at Pinochet's head, I will stand between him and the would-be assassin. The gunfire, instead of reaching him, will leave its imprint on the bullet-proof glass of his vehicle in the shape of my likeness. General Pinochet is my master, as is General Mendoza, Chief of Police, and I am here to tell you, in spite of my right-wing pigness, that your weathered little yellow wooden house is with you. It is with you with its salvaged packed-up trinkets and covered furniture. It is with you with its Diaguita blankets and copper artwork on the walls. It is with you with its wild pink rose bush by the door watered on hot days by the boy across the way, and the yellow used Citroën parked in the dirt driveway. It is with you with its sealed windows looking out onto the muddy Patagonian lane. Even with your books burned by the soldiers, with the ripped-open mattresses, with the sound of you girls weeping, it is with you. And your white stucco house is with you with its uncomfortable couch found abandoned in a west-side alleyway, with its metal shelf discovered by the UBC Physics Department dumpster, with its red Coma-Caca poster in the shape of a Coke bottle tacked above the toilet and sketch of Ho Chi Minh over the Salvation Army–orange dining-room table and the photo of Allende bearing arms on the day of the coup hanging in the hallway.

Beat.

Your two houses are in your inner house, with its emerald-green heart the size of your fist pumping seven thousand litres of blood per day through its four chambers, and its electric brain sending messages through its eighty-six billion neurons. Your inner house like Earth in miniature,

137

what with the light in your eyes, with your forests of
hair, with your valleys and mountains, your bubbling hot
springs and rivers and oceans, your thirty trillion cells
like whole galaxies housing your outer houses, those outer
houses pumping through your beating emerald heart right
now, crashing through the blue and green and purple
and red passageways of your inner house. I float here in
heaven before you as I step on the heads of those guilty
souls burning below us, as I stifle their screams and kick
at their arms threatening to pull me down to hell with my
babes in arms, and I witness you muscle your way through
your lives, spinning on your axis like the mini-planets that
you are, your joints popping from the magnet that pulls
you north, from the magnet that pulls you south at this
electrified border, with its barbed-wire wall desperately
trying to keep the South at bay, with its cameras and
search lights, its helicopters and shots ringing in the night,
with its brown ghosts and shrines. Your outer houses
are with you. Your outer houses are with you. In your
inner house.

*THE VIRGIN CARMEN disappears amid the
sound of static on the radio, which catches the
following snippets of verse mixed one after another:*

*from Ana Gabriel's version of Fernando
Maldonado's "Volver Volver": "Y volver volver, volver,
a tus brazos otra vez";*

*from Violeta Parra's "Qué pena siente el alma":
"Qué pena siente el alma, cuando la suerte impía, se
opone a los deseos, que anhela el corazón";*

*from Quilapayún's version of "¡Venceremos!":
"Venceremos, vencermos, mil cadenas habrá que*

138

romper, venceremos, venceremos, al fascismo
sabremos vencer";

finally leading into the top of McFadden &
Whitehead's "Ain't No Stopping Us Now."

The piece of highway that the family is travelling on breaks off and they are left rudderless, floating who knows where.

"Ain't No Stopping Us Now" plays in full, through the curtain call.

THE END

POST-SHOW MUSIC

Mujer
performed by Amparo Ochoa

A Cochabamba me voy
performed by Victor Jara

DISCOGRAPHY

Ballard Jr., Clint. "You're No Good." Track 1 on Linda Ronstadt, *Heart like a Wheel*. Capitol Records ST-11358, 1974.

Casey, Warren, and Jim Jacobs. "We Go Together." Track 22 on Various Artists, *Grease: The Original Soundtrack from the Motion Picture*. RSO RS-2-4002, 1978.

Cohen, Jerry, Gene McFadden, and John Whitehead. "Ain't No Stopping Us Now." Track 1 on McFadden & Whitehead, *McFadden & Whitehead*. Philadelphia International Records JZ 35800, 1979.

Fox, Charles, and Paul Williams. "The Love Boat." Track 1 on Jack Jones, *Nobody Does It Better*. MGM Records MG-1-5023, 1979.

Gamble, Kenneth, Cary Gilbert, and Leon Huff. "Don't Leave Me This Way." Track 1 on Thelma Houston, *Any Way You Like It*. Tamia Records T6-345S1, 1976.

Henley, Don, Glenn Frey, and J.D. Souther. "New Kid in Town." Track 2 on Eagles, *Hotel California*. Asylum Records 7E-1084, 1976.

Ittura, Claudio, and Sergio Ortega. "Venceremos." Track A on Quilapayún, *Venceremos* (single). Dicap JJS-110, 1971.

Jackson, Chuck, and Marvin Yancy. "This Will Be (An Everlasting Love)." Track 5 on Natalie Cole, *Inseparable*. Capitol Records ST-11429, 1975.

Jara, Victor. "A Cochabamba me voy." Track 12 on Victor Jara, *Pongo en tus manos abiertas*. Jota Jota JJL-03, 1969.

Lynn, Cheryl, David Foster, and David Paich. "Got to Be Real." Track 1 on Cheryl Lynn, *Cheryl Lynn*. Columbia Records JC 35486, 1978.

Maldonado, Fernando. "Volver, Volver." Track 3 on Ana Gabriel, *Tradicional*. Sony Music 2 516671, 2004.

Manzanero, Armando. "Esta tarde vi llover." Track 1 on Armando Manzanero, *Esta tarde vi llover*. RCA Victor 3-10258, 1967.

McCartney, Paul. "With a Little Luck." Track 9 on Wings, *London Town*. MPL (2) PAS 10012, OC 064-60 521, 1978.

McCoy, Van. "The Hustle." Track 3 on Van McCoy & the Soul City Symphony, *Disco Baby*. Avco AV-69006-698, 1975.

McKay, Al, Allee Willis, and Maurice White. "September." Track 7 on Earth, Wind & Fire, *The Best of Earth, Wind & Fire, Vol. 1*. ARC (3) / Columbia Records FC 35647, 1978.

Mtume, James, and Reggie Lucas. "Never Knew Love like This Before." Track 1 on Stephanie Mills, *Sweet Sensation*. 20th Century Fox Records T-603, 1980.

Ochoa, Amparo. "Mujer." Track 1 on Amparo Ochoa, *Mujer*. Discos Pueblos DP-1053, 1976.

Parra, Violetta. "Qué pena siente el alma." Track 1 on *Violetta Parra*. Odéon Records E-50040, 1955.

Perren, Freddie, and Keni St. Lewis. "Heaven Must Be Missing an Angel." Track 4 on Tavares, *Sky High!* Capitol Records ST-11533, 1976.

Redding, Otis. "Respect." Track 1 on Aretha Franklin, *I Never Loved a Man the Way I Love You*. Atlantic Records 8139, 1967.

Sayer, Leo, and Vini Poncia. "You Make Me Feel like Dancing." Track 2 on Leo Sayer, *Endless Flight*. Chrysalis CHR 1125, 1976.

Temperton, Rod. "Rock with You." Track 2 on Michael Jackson, *Off the Wall*. Epic FE 35745, 1979.

White, Barry. "Let the Music Play." Track 6 on Barry White, *Let the Music Play*. 20th Century Fox Records T-502, 1976.

———. "Love's Theme." Track 1 on Love Unlimited, *Under the Influence of ... Love Unlimited*. 20th Century Fox Records T-414, 1973.

White, Maurice, and Wayne Vaughn. "Let's Groove." Track 1 on Earth, Wind & Fire, *Raise!* Arc (3) / Columbia Records TC 37548, 1981.

Whitfield, Norman. "Car Wash." Track 1 on Rose Royce, *Car Wash: Original Motion Picture Soundtrack*. MCA Records MCA2-6000, 1976.

Williams, John. "Star Wars Theme / Cantina Band." Track 7 on Meco, *Music Inspired by Star Wars and Other Galactic Funk*. Millennium, Casablanca MNLP 8001, 1977.

Willis, Allee, with Jon Lind. "Boogie Wonderland." Track 5 (with the Emotions) on Earth, Wind & Fire, *I Am*. ARC (3) / Columbia Records FC 35730, 1979.

ACKNOWLEDGMENTS

Eternal gratitude to my artistic home, Electric Company Theatre, for developing and premiering this play. I think it's pretty safe to say that no other theatre in Canada would have done so. I have written other plays, such as *The Refugee Hotel*, that were meant to live on a mainstage. In my thirty years in the business, this is the first time that one of my plays has landed there. Thank you to the Vancouver Playhouse for hosting us.

Thanks also to Vancouver's Playwrights Theatre Centre for developing and being associate producer of the premiere, and to the British Columbia Arts Council, rice and beans theatre, November Theatre, and the Banff Playwrights Lab for developmental support.

There are not enough words that can express my thanks to Electric Company's artistic producer, Clayton Baraniuk, my dramaturge Heidi Taylor, and my director Juliette Carrillo. Their fierce support and advocacy for this play made it what it is.

And to every single actor, director, audience member, and colleague along the way who gave invaluable feedback at every reading and workshop, and to the actors, artistic team, and crew of the world premiere. Thank you.

PHOTO: ALEJANDRA AGUIRRE

Carmen Aguirre is a Chilean Canadian, award-winning theatre artist and author who has written and co-written over twenty-five plays, including *Chile Con Carne and Other Early Works*, *The Refugee Hotel*, *The Trigger*, *Blue Box*, and *Broken Tailbone*, as well as the number one international bestseller *Something Fierce: Memoirs of a Revolutionary Daughter* (winner of CBC Canada Reads 2012), and its bestselling sequel, *Mexican Hooker #1 and My Other Roles Since the Revolution*. She is currently writing an adaptation of Euripides's *Medea*, commissioned by Vancouver's Rumble Theatre, Molière's *The Learned Ladies* for Toronto's Factory Theatre, a short digital piece for Ontario's Stratford Festival entitled *Floating Life*, and an untitled play on the life of famed twentieth-century Italian photographer and revolutionary Tina Modotti for Vancouver's Electric Company Theatre. *Reframed*, an outdoor performance piece about online discourse, conceived and co-created with the Electric Company, received its world premiere on October 7, 2020, in Vancouver, commissioned by Ottawa's National Arts Centre for its Grand Acts of Theatre initiative. Carmen is a Core Artist at Electric Company Theatre, a co-founding member of the Canadian Latinx Theatre Artist Coalition (CALTAC), and has over eighty film, TV, and stage acting credits, including her award-winning lead role in the Canadian premiere of Stephen Adly Guirgis's *The Motherfucker with the Hat*, and her Leo-nominated lead performance in the independent feature film *Bella Ciao!* She looks forward to starring in Cecilia Araneda's stunning debut feature film *Intersection*, to be shot in Winnipeg in spring 2021, and in the Canadian premiere of Melinda Lopez's one-woman show, *Mala*, at Vancouver's Arts Club Theatre. Carmen was a finalist for the 2020 Siminovitch Prize, the most prestigious theatre award in Canada. She is a graduate of Studio 58. carmenaguirre.ca